IT
HAPPENS
ALL THE
TIME

CHARLES & BECKY McQUAIG

rue Accounts of Miracles in Our Day

IT HAPPENS ALL THE TIME

STORIES OF

HEALING • PROVISION • PROTECTION
ANGELIC VISITATION • DIVINE INTERVENTION

It Happens All the Time

by Charles and Becky McQuaig

© 1998, Word Aflame Press
Hazelwood, MO 63042-2299

Cover Design by Paul Povolni

Printed in United States of America

Printed by

WORD AFLAME® PRESS
8855 DUNN ROAD
HAZELWOOD, MO 63042-2299

Library of Congress Cataloging-in-Publication Data

It happens all the time : true accounts of miracles in our day : stories of healing, provision, protection, angelic visitation, and divine intervention / [compiled by] Charles and Becky McQuaig.
     p.   cm.
   ISBN 1-56722-223-4
    1. Miracles—Case studies. 2. Providence and government of God—Case studies. I. McQuaig, Charles. II. McQuaig, Becky.
BT97.2.I8 1998
231.7'3—dc21   98-39131
                                          CIP

Dedication

We dedicate this book to all those who have given of their time and effort to contribute their testimonies to the glory of God. Because of their willingness to expose their personal experiences to open scrutiny, we are able to see the hand of God manifested in ways not readily acknowledged by the human spirit.

We also dedicate this book to our own personal *miracle*, our daughter, Whitney McQuaig. It is our hope that she will see, with spiritual eyes, God's works and involvement in our everyday lives and embrace the fact that "It Happens All The Time!"

Contents

Foreword

This book is composed of testimonies of people who have experienced angelic visitations, miraculous healings, phenomenal occurrences, and God's marvelous intervention in critical situations.

It is written and compiled by two beautiful, dedicated, talented people, husband and wife: Charles and Becky McQuaig.

Because they have experienced several miraculous incidences in their own lives, they are committed to making people aware of God's involvement in our day-to-day situations and giving Him the credit He deserves. Upon reading these stories, you will see, as I have, that miracles are quite common; in fact, they happen all the time.

Becky and Charlie, thanks for bringing this to our attention and thanks for being such wonderful friends.

Marie Bush

Acknowledgements

We especially thank Sherry Dye of Greenville, South Carolina, who did much of our editing. Sherry, you'll never know how much we appreciate the countless hours you've put in and your patience with us over the past two and a half years while we arranged and rearranged this book. God could not have given us a better sister and sister-in-law. We love you.

In loving memory, we wish to honor three very special people who gave us their stories but have since gone to be with the Lord. They were all personal friends and are greatly missed. We trust their testimonies of victory will be an inspiration and build the faith of future generations:

D. L. Welch: founder and former pastor of the First Pentecostal Church in Pensacola, Florida

Sarah Elizabeth Brown: our adopted grandmother and prayer partner (referred to in "Healings" story by Suzi Smith)

Estelle Hurst: faithful Christian friend and mentor

For their lives and their testimonies, we give thanks.

Introduction

My daughter, Whitney, and I share a very special part of every day in what we call snuggle time. At the end of the evening, when homework is finished, baths are taken, and toys are put away, we fluff up the pillows and crawl right in the middle of my big feather mattress, eager to dissect the events of the day. We cover every topic, from the bird nest in the bush by the playground to the fat content in a cream cheese brownie.

Often during this time together, Whitney will ask me to tell her the story of how God healed my hand when I was a little girl. (You'll read the story later in the book.) Though she knows the story by heart, she loves to hear it over and over again. We have shared so many wonderful stories that by age eight she knows that when we're sick God is our healer. When we have a need, He is our provider. She knows that He is our deliverer in time of trouble, and above all, He is our Savior.

I started writing down the stories I've shared with her so she will have them in years to come, especially if I'm not around to tell them. Then I decided to gather stories from some of my friends.

As the stories came in, I was overwhelmed at God's involvement in every aspect of our lives. This curiosity provoked me to research the Scriptures. I quickly found evidence of God's interest in all we do, both great and small. Not only did I discover His interest but also His desire for us to trust in Him for direction, protection, and provision.

Trust in the LORD with all thine heart; and lean not unto thine own understanding. In all thy ways acknowledge him, and he shall direct thy paths (Proverbs 3:5-6).

He shall cover thee with his feathers, and under his wings shalt thou trust: his truth shall be thy shield and buckler (Psalm 91:4).

And thine ears shall hear a word behind thee, saying, This is the way, walk ye in it, when ye turn to the right hand, and when ye turn to the left (Isaiah 30:21).

I will instruct thee and teach thee in the way which thou shalt go: I will guide thee with mine eye (Psalm 32:8).

Ask, and it shall be given you; seek, and ye shall find; knock, and it shall be opened unto you (Matthew 7:7).

Whatever the need, we, as God's children, have an open invitation to come before Him:

Let us therefore come boldly unto the throne of grace, that we may obtain mercy, and find grace to help in time of need (Hebrews 4:16).

I want my child to understand this principle. It doesn't matter the nature of the problem. God is able to help and eagerly awaits the opportunity to do so.

Whitney is blessed to have a strong Christian heritage of several generations, both maternal and paternal, but many children and adults do not share that benefit. If you fall into that category, this book is for you too. You may not have glorious testimonies that have been passed down to you from previous generations, but we are all joint heirs of God through Christ (Romans 8:16-17).

This means we share a common heritage. Each of our experiences benefits all of us as we glorify God as one body, the church of the living God. We should share these experiences to build memorials for future generations and constantly remind those who come behind us of God's faithfulness.

Becky McQuaig

1

Healing

Back in the days before air conditioning had become a standard fixture in homes, large window fans were used. As children, my two sisters and I spent weekends with my grandparents so we could attend church.

One Sunday morning, the weather was hot and muggy. My grandmother was at the opposite end of the house when she called for my grandfather to plug in the kitchen fan. My grandfather had stepped outside to feed his hunting dogs and did not hear her request.

I took matters into my own hands. Though I was only five years old, I remember the incident vividly.

The outlet exploded as I plugged in the fan. An intense flash of fire charred my right hand, causing what I know now to be second- and third-degree burns. Screaming in pain, I watched my skin shrivel and melt.

In horror my grandparents grabbed me up and rushed me to the hospital. Granny wet her little flowered handkerchief and quickly wrapped my hand as she continually prayed, "In Jesus' name, help this baby, Lord."

There was no such thing as 911, and cars didn't go as fast as they do now, but Ol' Spittin' Jenny, as we called their car, traveled as fast as she ever did.

Thankfully, the route to Baptist Hospital took us right in front of our church, where Pastor D. L. Welch and Brother Childress, who later pastored in Jacksonville, Florida, were standing in the parking lot, talking. My grandfather stopped the car and rushed me to the men of God to be prayed for. Within seconds I hushed my crying in amazement that the pain had stopped.

I unfolded Granny's flowered handkerchief to see my hand. I wasn't surprised to see a normal hand, because I was told God healed, and I believed it.

I'm glad my grandparents had more faith in God than they did in the doctors at the emergency room. I do know the recovery time is a lot shorter when we take our ailments to Dr. Jesus.

The first time my mother can recall witnessing a miracle was around 1949 when my older sister, Suzi, was a baby. Suzi was very sick with a fever of 103 degrees. Pastor Welch came to the house to pray for her. About two minutes after he prayed, my grandmother took her temperature again. It had dropped from 103 degrees to a normal temperature in that short length of time.

Unfortunately, with advances in medical technology and "better living through chemistry," we find that our society as a whole is less dependent on God for healing. If we have a headache, we get an aspirin. If we have indigestion, we simply pop in an antacid tablet. Should we have a more complicated problem, we see our physician and obtain a prescription or other treatment.

There is nothing wrong with obtaining assistance from doctors, hospitals, and medicine. I am a nurse, and I thank God for the knowledge that He has blessed all of us in the medical profession with to help people. The problem comes when we put more faith in the "mechanic" than in the Maker, and that is what most people seem to do today.

Working in a large medical complex, I am amazed at the number of people entering each day. The central file room is filled from floor to ceiling with row after row of individual files, so that there is little space for personnel to work, and new patients register daily.

How many people would find the answer to their problems if they would only read their instruction manual—the Word of God? A large number of ailments are the direct result of worry, bitterness, and the failure to follow biblical health principles.

A prime example is the Bible's teaching on learning to control anger. Psalm 37:8 says, "Cease from anger, and forsake wrath: fret not thyself in any wise to do evil." Proverbs 15:1 tells us, "A soft answer turneth away wrath: but grievous words stir up anger." Doctors say that anger can cause an elevation in blood pressure, gastric upset, and headaches. Prolonged problems in this area may even lead to ulcers and heart attacks.

Most people know that tobacco use contributes to lung cancer and that alcohol consumption leads to liver dysfunction, but it is also medically proven that people who both smoke and drink have a far greater risk of contracting throat cancer than those who do only one or the other. Both practices are obvious abuses to our bodies, and I Corinthians 3:17 emphatically warns us, "If any man defile the temple of God, him shall God destroy; for the temple of God is holy, which temple ye are." In Leviticus 11-15, God gave the Israelites detailed instructions on diet, personal hygiene, and purification techniques. I Corinthians 6-7 stress the necessity for sexual abstinence before marriage and monogamy thereafter. Following this teaching is the best solution to the problem of sexually transmitted diseases, including AIDS.

The bottom line is this: our society could avoid, minimize, or eliminate many of our ailments if we would only apply God's principles. Of course, not all illness is preventable. Many times, God allows an infirmity in order to manifest His works (John 9:3). We should also remember that whether or not God heals a certain person at a certain time, He is no less a healer.

Becky McQuaig

When my oldest son, Tom, was four years old, I left him with a baby-sitter one Saturday while I did a little shopping. When I returned, she mentioned that another child had thrown an oyster shell at Tommy, and it had hit him in the eye.

At first sight I knew it was a serious injury as blood had begun pooling in the iris of his eye. I rushed him to the hospital at once, with flashers and horn going all the way there.

He was immediately sedated, and we were told he must remain that way for the first three days.

He was fed intravenously so he could remain perfectly still through the critical period. If the blood subsided, the eye could heal itself, but if after the third day it had blackballed, where the vessels bleed and flood the eye, they would remove the eye.

After the third day, to our horror, the eye had blackballed, and enucleation of the eye was scheduled.

We prayed desperately and asked churches over the country to help us pray. My brother, Ellis Myers of Melbourne, Florida, anointed Tom with oil and prayed.

The eye miraculously began to clear. The doctors and nurses could not believe it. They remarked that it just could not happen, but it did!

The ophthalmologist examined Tom two weeks after he was discharged from the hospital. He said the bloodstain on the iris would discolor his beautiful blue eye, and it would never look the same again. He also recommended annual testing for glaucoma.

That was twenty-five years ago, and the eye is perfect with no discoloration and no glaucoma. We are thrilled, and we still thank the Lord for His bountiful blessings!

Marie Bush

While my son and I were on our way to church, he pointed out to me several ugly warts located on both hands. He told me that while he was visiting his grandparents, his grandfather had taken him down to the creek to conjure his warts away. He did it using a mixture of certain kind of leaves and water. By my son's admission, however, the procedure didn't work, for it had been quite a long time prior.

I told my son we needed to ask Jesus to heal the warts; He could do it. We then prayed and asked the Lord to heal my son of this problem. A few weeks after that my son said to me, "Look at my hands, Dad. The warts are all gone."

This was a valuable lesson of faith that has stuck with my son and me until this day and continually serves to uplift our faith. He was around ten years old at the time and today is almost thirty-five. Jesus also healed my wife of breast cancer in 1976.

John E. Jackson

Over forty years ago, I was diagnosed with cancer in my lower abdomen. My doctor explained to me that the biopsy was positive, and immediate surgery to remove the tumor was indicated.

I decided to go to a meeting where an evangelist was having special prayer for the sick. I was prayed for and was immediately healed.

My surgeon verified that the tumor was no longer present and even told me, "God did a miracle." I am seventy-eight years old now and still free of cancer!

Estelle Hurst

When my granddaughter, Cynthia, was about six years old, I rushed her to the doctor because of a severe cold and acute tonsillitis. Her throat was swelling, obstructing her airway. The doctor said he would have to do an emergency procedure to remove the obstruction. I started crying and pleading the name of Jesus. Suddenly, she began to breathe easier. The doctor didn't know what to say. She continued to improve and just kept on getting better. I thank Jesus for being there when I needed Him. He truly is my best friend.

Angie Finney

In January 1991 Anthony and I found out we were going to have a baby. This event was unexpected but very welcome.

My pregnancy started with the normal three to four months of morning sickness. Then around July, I started gaining too much weight and showed signs of toxemia. In the middle of July, I started having a minor pain, which my doctor passed off as heartburn, and he gave me the medicine he thought I needed.

On the mornings of August 10 and 11, I called my doctor because the pain was increasing, and again he told me to take the same medicine. Finally, on August 12, I called again. This time the pain was even more severe. I was told to come to the hospital immediately.

When I arrived at the hospital, I went to a room that quickly filled with doctors, nurses, machines, and family. As many as five specialists examined me at one time. After they did an ultrasound, they determined that the baby was developed enough to be taken.

My doctor quietly whispered to Anthony the necessity of doing so. He told Anthony that I had toxemia and my liver had stopped functioning; therefore, the baby was not getting nourishment and was losing weight. He also said, "If we wait another day you will have to decide between the baby's life and the mother's life." We then gave the doctor permission to take the baby by cesarean section.

They took me to the operating room, where Anthony was allowed to hold my hand through surgery. The doctor gave the baby and me only a twenty-five-percent chance of survival.

When I held my baby for the first time, I told her she was my miracle baby. My doctor agreed and said we must have had people praying for us. He also commented that God obviously had plans for us, for the odds had been against us. My doctor had not seen a pregnancy like this in twenty-five years.

Shortly after we were released from the hospital, we heard of two other ladies with the same problem. In one case the baby did not survive, and the mother's outcome was still uncertain.

Our odds of living were very slim. However, God stepped in and gave us a wonderfully healthy (though tiny) baby girl, weighing only four pounds thirteen ounces. We named our baby Christine Elizabeth, after my two grandmothers.

I thank God for the parents he allowed Anthony and me to have. Tom, Sandra, Gaynor, and Earlene are parents whose first priority is to teach their children the ways of God. We want to teach Christine the ways of God just as our parents are teaching us.

Thank You, Jesus, for this golden opportunity!

Vicki Perkins

As a little girl, I burned my right hand severely

with hot cooking oil. My mother immediately began praying for me. She did not apply any medication but prayed about two hours. I was hurting very badly, but the hurting stopped. I healed with no blisters, scar, or any trace of the burn whatsoever.

This was a manifestation of God's healing power to me. This healing, as a child, prepared me to come through a greater affliction in my adult life: cancer.

I couldn't believe it when my doctor told me that I had it. I told the doctor that God could heal me, and I felt that He would. I had the best doctors and facilities, God on my side, and a great church family that was praying daily for me. I didn't feel that I had finished everything that God had for me to do.

I took eight treatments of chemotherapy, one treatment every three weeks. My cancer cell count came down. I was monitored very closely. After only two months, my count rose again, and the tumor began to grow.

This time I received more aggressive therapy. I had to be admitted to the hospital once a month for six days, during which I received treatments every twenty-four hours. I went through this procedure for four months. I became very weak and sick and lost all my hair. My oncologist decided to stop treatment and reevaluate my condition because nothing up to that point had helped.

In the doctors' opinion, the chemotherapy was only killing me. They told me that they would try to keep my quality of life as high as possible for however long I might have. I just shook my head, still not believing what they were telling me.

My cousin Betty was with me that day, so I told her I wanted to talk with my pastor, Paul Welch. I explained to him what I had been told. He was very compassionate but wasn't able to give me the comfort I wanted. Deep down, I knew God would be my real comfort.

I never gave up. One Wednesday night after church, Pastor Welch came to speak to me and shake my hand. I said, "When the doctors and man give up on you, that's when God will take over and do His miraculous works." Brother Welch agreed, "That's right! Amen."

I am a living, walking testimony of that fact. I went back four weeks later for blood work and my progress report. My doctor told me the tumor was gone and my blood work was normal. No cancer! I said right then and there, "Thank You, Jesus."

That has been a year and a half ago. My hair came back curly. God gives me many opportunities to tell of His wondrous work in my life. I am very thankful and feel that this is now my purpose in life. God is still the same yesterday, today, and forever. If it is God's will, He can and will heal you, too!

Mary Milstead

During a testimony service in Covington, Georgia,

I requested prayer for a tumor that had been diagnosed and could only be removed surgically. At the
time I was seven months pregnant. The doctor said the
tumor would double in size during pregnancy. A lady
in the congregation said she felt that if I would go forward for prayer, I would be healed, so I did.

After childbirth, the doctor was surprised to find
that the tumor was small. Six weeks later he checked
again and found no trace of the tumor. God had
removed it! To God be the glory.

Many times since then God has healed me. I've
had moles just fall off. A growth on my hand disappeared in just one day. There has never been a time in
my life that God has not rescued me. Behold, God is!

Billie Jean Kobold

Some years ago, I had a mass in my knee that
bothered me quite a bit. One night in a Pentecostal service in Molino, Florida, I was prayed for. When I
awoke the next morning, the mass was gone. I knew
that I was healed by God.

Ralph Reid

After seven years of marriage and multiple infer-
tility problems, God blessed us with our first child. Gil

and I had promised God that if He blessed us with a child, we would dedicate the baby back to Him. This is a Christian way of offering back to the Lord a baby to safeguard in His keeping until that child is accountable for his own spiritual walk with God.

In 1977 when our daughter, Jennifer, was born, my obstetrician referred to her as "a miracle," because he knew our problems and how desperately we had tried to have a child. Deep down inside, we felt that God had smiled on us, honoring my mother-in-law's prayer for us. From that time forward, we were blessed abundantly. Two more daughters followed: Lynn, then Julie. We went from no children and "infertile" to a family of five in five years. My doctor was amazed that conception had occurred at all since he surgically observed dual problems—each problem within itself enough to prevent pregnancy.

Little did we know, as parents, how much we would have to depend on God, especially through accidents, sickness, and the tough times that were ahead. We found Lynn cold, lifeless, and blue in her bath water at the age of eleven months. I left her older sister with her, but she left the room shortly after I did without my knowledge. When I returned, Lynn was lifeless. Just the same, God watched over her and allowed her dad to resuscitate that little blue body!

After Life Flight took her to the hospital to have her stomach pumped, she was diagnosed as normal, not suffering any brain damage at all. Today it is rare if she doesn't make the honor roll at school.

When Jennifer, my oldest child, was six years old, the Lord was again with us. We went through a tough illness that her pediatrician thought was a virus. After several days of not keeping food down, she was hospitalized with dehydration. A bone marrow test revealed hemolytic uremic syndrome, which is a rare renal disease capable of shutting down the kidneys. Treatment requires a transplant.

Her kidneys were filtering only ten percent of her blood when the doctors performed an emergency blood transfusion. They advised us to look for a donor outside the family and plan to have kidneys of family members available in case of recurrence, which strikes usually in six-year intervals. They also told us that her weak kidneys would probably not be able to filter the new blood from the transfusion. A dialysis machine was on standby.

As the transfusion was in process, our pastor, Paul Welch, walked into her room and calmly prayed, "Lord, You take this blood, filter it, and let her body accept it, in Jesus' name!"

A miracle was performed! Later that night, Jenny sat up in bed and for the first time in eight days was hungry. God had given her a special touch. She never required a transplant.

A later test revealed that her kidneys were constantly improving. There is no record of this situation occurring in any previous case of this disease. All previous patients had to have transplants and later had recurrences.

Jenny is now sweet sixteen and perfectly healthy. Ten years have passed, and she has had no further problems with hemolytic uremic syndrome.

Our third little miracle, Julie, has never come near death or major sickness and has brought nothing to us but laughter, wit, and charm. She is a picture of health and is a hardworking child academically, physically, and spiritually. She is truly a gift from above.

Sometimes Gil and I feel we have overworked God and His angels by asking special protection in our little family of five, but it is our desire to give back to Him and His kingdom what He has given us.

We continually pray that God will use our girls however He sees fit! We are so thankful to be able to train up our children in the way they should go. Our goal and our miracle will conclude when all of us get to heaven.

Bobbie Richards

My eyesight failed, and within three days I was declared legally blind from optic neuritis. I was totally blind in my right eye and legally blind in my left eye. I spent thirty days in Barnes Hospital, St. Louis, Missouri.

Pastor Guy Roam and members of the Pentecostal church there began praying for me. The doctors told me that I would probably get some eyesight back in the left eye, but my right eye was hopeless. Thankfully, I had consulted the Great Physician.

After thirty days of brain x-rays, spinal taps, blood tests, and more, the doctors could not determine what caused the neuritis. All they could tell me was to expect blindness in my right eye and very little sight in my left.

When I was released from the hospital, my eyesight started to return! In about a week I had regained twenty-twenty vision and still have perfect eyesight.

When my doctors reexamined and questioned me, they said, "This just doesn't happen!" But happen it did! God had intervened!

Darvin Kobold

I was born with asthma. Many times it became so severe that my parents would take me to the hospital. They were told that there was no cure.

One night we went to a Pentecostal church service. The preacher didn't know us and was unaware of my health condition. The Lord revealed my condition to him, so he came back to our pew and prayed for me. God healed my asthma, and I was never bothered with it again.

Now God has healed my daughter Rachel of asthma. Truly God is a miracle worker!

Christine Reid

My dad, Ralph Jarman, was coming home very late one night from work when a car traveling in the opposite direction crossed the center line, causing him to swerve in order to avoid a head-on collision. Losing control of his convertible, he plummeted down a culvert and flipped end over end. He was not wearing his seat belt and was thrown from the car, only to have it fall back on top of him.

He sustained a major head injury, bilateral arm fractures, and several broken ribs. His lung was punctured when he was speared by a windshield wiper.

The road he was driving on was a small country road in Byron, Georgia. The area wasn't well populated, and the other car kept going. Fortunately, the accident occurred very close to the last house for several miles, and help was summoned.

My father was in critical condition. He went into full cardiac arrest three times. His respiratory insufficiency necessitated a tracheotomy. He was in the intensive care unit for three weeks in a coma.

He was a musician and singer, but there was little hope that he would recover to do either again. His prognosis, at best, was grim.

My little grandmother, his mother, began a prayer vigil. She refused to give up on her son or the promises of God. Day and night she prayed, along with others, for his complete recovery.

Within a few weeks, he was out of the coma. A few

more weeks and he was able to leave the hospital. Today he is singing and playing the piano just as before the accident.

I'm thankful to have a grandmother who refused to give up and extremely thankful to have my father back.

Barry Jarman

In 1975, I had headaches at least two or three days a week, each getting progressively worse. I would take every kind of pain medicine I could find. I went to the doctor, but nothing he gave me would help for very long.

One Sunday night, Ralph Glasgow was preaching at our church. I wanted to go so much, but I was too sick. I told my husband to go without me and have the people at church pray for me.

When he returned from church, he brought Brother Glasgow with him. Brother Glasgow sat down by the bed and began telling me about some wonderful things the Lord had done for him and other people he had prayed for. At that moment he said, "Sister Davis, we are going to command the headache to leave, never to come back, in the name of the Lord Jesus."

The headaches left and haven't returned. That was about nineteen years ago! I can't praise God enough.

Lottie Ezell Davis

Ten years ago I went through several days of nausea, which rapidly progressed into a serious, life-threatening situation. My protein dropped to a critical level, and the emergency room team could not palpate a pulse.

After temporarily stabilizing me, they began to do extensive testing with no conclusive diagnosis of my problem. Inexplicably, I began gaining weight, averaging ten pounds a day. I went from 130 to 195 pounds in less than a week.

Diuretics were useless. Nothing they did relieved the edema. I was slipping into congestive heart failure and could not so much as lift my body from a horizontal position. My legs were swollen to three times their normal size. I was actually dying, and they couldn't find out why.

Thankfully, I had a praying family and a praying church to intercede on my behalf.

One dear lady, Sarah Brown, whom I have known all my life, came up to the hospital, laid hands on me, and prayed for me. This lady is a dedicated Christian, full of the Spirit, and I have confidence in her prayers.

Immediately, I began to improve. I lost the weight more rapidly than I had gained it! Within two days I was home.

The doctors were never able to diagnosis my condition, but that really is unimportant to me. God is the healer of all our diseases, even the ones that have no name!

Suzi Smith

Being in ill health with diabetes and arthritis, I did not have an average life. Where other people can jump out of bed and grab a cup of coffee in the morning, I had pain and much difficulty getting out of bed. My life consisted of living from pill to pill and wondering when my next emergency shot of insulin would come.

I took plenty of pills for the pain. I took Valium for my nerves, estrogen for my hormones, pills for my arthritis, pills for everything. I took pain pills, as much as four at a time just to ease the hurt. I was in and out of the hospital, unable to control my sugar count. I was getting worse. I had ulcers right under my ribs, my hips were deteriorating from the inside out, and the doctor informed me that arthritis was spreading to my spine. I would get up at 3:00 A.M. to get a shot because my sugar count had gone up so high. Sometimes my sugar count would drop so low that I didn't know what I was doing or saying or even who I was! I was in so much pain that I couldn't concentrate. I didn't know what life was without drugs and doctors.

Occasionally I drank, but alcohol messes up the blood sugar. The effect two beers would have on the average person would be equivalent to a six-pack if I drank them. When people have diabetes as I had, they don't drink much unless they want to die.

When it rained I was in bed for weeks at a time. I was not a happy person and definitely not somebody you would want to be with. I was always irritable and tired. I didn't know what it was like to hold my children without being in extreme pain. I used a wheelchair most of the time because it hurt to walk. My doctor told me it wouldn't be long until I would be in it on a permanent basis.

My fiancé was looking for a job. While he was going through the phone book, an ad caught his attention. He called the number and got the job.

About a week later, his boss, Scott Mulholand, came to our house. The conversation somehow turned into a discussion about God. By the end of the visit, I had a hunger inside that I had never experienced before. I wanted to know God and earnestly desired to be filled with His Spirit.

I had been told that God heals people, but I didn't think He would heal me. I said, "There's no way; I've been sick for sixteen years and can't believe God would suddenly make things better." Little did I know that my life was about to change drastically!

My fiancé, Shane, came home from work one day and said he wanted us to go to church with Scott. We went during the church's sixtieth anniversary celebration. I found myself even hungrier for God. We went again on Father's Day, but when we got home, all we could do was fight. There were no nice words between us. I couldn't think of one nice thing to say to the man.

I called Scott's wife, Tina, and told her what was happening. She said we needed to pray together because the devil was not happy at all. Apparently he did not want to lose another follower.

I didn't understand what was going on inside of me, but I knew I was a total wreck—mentally, physically, and emotionally. When we returned to church, the pastor asked everyone to come down front and pray. I knew I had nothing to lose. I was already a mess.

When I went to pray, Scott came over, anointed me with oil, and started praying for me. I could hear people talking, but it seemed their voices were fading away. The most awesome, wonderful peace came over me. My soul quit aching; my heart felt as if it were skipping beats. There was no pain. I started shaking all over. I was really shaking! I started speaking in a language I didn't understand. Then a tingling started from the bottom of my feet and went all the way to the top of my head. The experience I had was just like in the second chapter of Acts, where people were filled with the Holy Ghost.

The next morning, I bounced out of bed like a jumping bean. This time there was no pain!

I was later baptized in Jesus' name. God took away all of my pain, all of my diabetes, and all of my arthritis. I thank Him daily for His gift. My life is just like the song: "I once was lost but now am found," and it's glorious! Glory be to God!

Virginia May Perdue

My daughter, Robin, went to the beach alone one day to have some quiet time and to read. She was on her stomach enjoying the warmth of the sunshine and taking a little nap when she was abruptly awakened by a man sitting on her back.

The attacker began beating her in the head with a heavy, blunt object that the police later determined to be a hammer or tire tool. Her assailant dragged her unconscious body behind the sand dunes.

A marine had been jogging along the beach and noticed Robin as he passed. When he came back by, he was startled to see her belongings scattered in a path leading to the dunes. He decided to investigate. He found her bloody, beaten body in the sand and, from the absence of vital signs, assumed she was dead.

At the same time, in a classroom, one of Robin's friends from church, Karen Anglin, felt compelled to pray for Robin. Karen didn't know why but could not disregard her strong feelings.

The marine left Robin and ran to the road to flag down help. The man who stopped happened to be a park ranger, and he called for emergency services instantly over his two-way radio.

The police arrived and roped off the area, also thinking Robin had been murdered, and began a search for clues. Eventually someone touched her body and she moved. They could not believe it. Life

Flight was called, and she was airlifted to Baptist Hospital in Pensacola.

Dr. A. B. Sisco, the neurosurgeon on call that day, just happened to be in the hospital when Robin arrived. She was rushed into surgery with massive head injuries. She sustained six skull fractures, one of which was indented, causing a serious brain laceration in the area controlling speech and motor functions.

Dr. Sisco came out of surgery and inquired which was her dominant hand so the level of brain damage could be determined later. When told she was an accomplished pianist, he simply shook his head and said, "Poor thing." There was certainty on his part that her musical career was over.

Though her words were confused and she was unable to say what she was thinking, she never became frustrated or angry. A few days after the injury, she tried to write me a note. The only part I could understand was "Dear Mom" and "I love you."

One week later she wrote me another note. This time she was completely coherent, and I could read everything she was writing. Each day was a miracle. Her recovery was astonishing. She was hospitalized only three days.

A short time after she came home, our pastor, Paul Welch, brought a visiting evangelist, Lee Stoneking, to our home to pray for Robin. Brother Stoneking asked if she thought she could play the piano. Bravely, she approached the instrument she loved so well and began to play Chopin.

To look at my precious daughter with her scarred, shaven head and see this girl who had just a few days prior been thought dead, now playing the piano, how could I or anyone else doubt that the healing hand of God had touched her? Robin truly is a miracle child.

She was scheduled to begin college a week after her accident but for obvious reasons had to cancel. She did, however, begin the very next quarter. She was to take Differential Equations but could not quite handle that level of math, so she dropped back to repeat Calculus 3 that term and went on to make an "A" in Differential Equations the next term! She was a little upset about having to repeat Calculus 3 until we pointed out that most people never get to that level in the first place.

The man who attacked Robin was a suspected serial killer in the murders of seven girls, all of whom looked very much like Robin and all of whom were killed near water. The differences were that he had disfigured the other seven girls' faces while Robin's was untouched, and he had strangled the others after beating them.

No one knows why he did not strangle or disfigure Robin. There was, however, a gentleman in that area with a metal detector, and the noise he caused may have frightened the assailant away. Perhaps he saw the marine coming by. We may never know.

Today, eight years later, Robin is married with two beautiful little boys. She teaches home school courses and piano.

Another miracle is how quickly Robin's hair grew

after surgery. Within a year, it was down to the middle of her back, and now it is below her waist. People ask her if she has ever cut her hair and can't believe that eight years ago she was bald!

Lola Richardson

It was February 2, 1993, and I was in my Florida room trying out my new four-foot-deep hot tub. Attempting to get out, I rose up to sit on the side and lost my balance, flipping backwards and landing on my head. I broke my neck and three toes in the fall. The pain was unbearable!

The nearest phone was in my bedroom, which was several yards away. I was alone, terrified, and unable to call for help. I slipped in and out of consciousness several times because of the pain. I don't know how, because I was partially paralyzed, but I somehow managed to drag myself into the bedroom and pull the phone off the nightstand.

My right arm was totally useless; I could only function with my left. As I reached for the phone, I heard my neck crunch, and I passed out again. I woke up some time later saying, "God, help me!" Looking at the clock, I couldn't believe I had been on the floor from six o'clock the night before till five o'clock the next morning.

I was so disoriented that I couldn't think to dial

911. Instead, I called my neighbor and told her I had broken my neck and needed help. She called the ambulance for me and rushed over to my house.

It took the paramedics forty minutes to stabilize my neck in order to transport me to the hospital. I had a C 6-7 neck fracture. Both of my doctors said it was a miracle that I survived the fall with this particular type of neck injury. Apparently, most patients die instantly.

I was in tong traction with screws in my head for five days. I stayed in the hospital only two weeks. I then wore a brace for three months and went through much physical therapy, but all that is of little consequence considering that God restored full use of my arms and legs.

I know without a doubt that the prayers of my friends and family sustained me through this whole ordeal.

Mary Frances Kent

In February of 1982 my brother and I were deer hunting. As I climbed into the truck to leave, his gun went off. It was a fifty-four-caliber, black-powder gun. The shot went through my left foot, coming out the bottom side and blowing most of my foot away.

He rushed me to West Florida Regional Medical Center, where Dr. Stephen Beissinger was on call. My brother made a few phone calls, and within thirty minutes between fifty and sixty people arrived at the hospital. They began to pray as I went into surgery.

While I was under anesthesia, Dr. Beissinger went out to my family. He told them the damage was too severe for him to save the foot, and he would need to amputate. My wife and father signed the consent giving permission to cut off my foot.

When he returned to the operating room, the doctor decided instead to clean up the foot and see if there was any conceivable way to save it. He spent five and a half hours picking out bone fragments, pieces of my boot, and particles from the bullet.

I stayed in the hospital five days, during which time the doctor decided that amputation was indicated after all. I signed the necessary papers and went back to surgery. Once I got back in there, the doctor decided to try one more thing. In an effort to reconstruct, he took a bone graft from my hip and placed it in my foot, then took skin from my leg to cover the exposed underlying tissue. He warned me that should the bone graft break, little else could be done. Three weeks after the surgery, I walked out of the hospital in a cast but with two feet.

Between two and three years later, I was walking across the yard when the bone graft snapped. The pain was excruciating.

I went back to Dr. Beissinger, who reviewed the x-rays with me. They showed a separation in the bone about the size of a pencil. He said there was nothing else to do but amputate.

This was on a Friday. Since I pastored a church in

Mississippi and needed to make arrangements to cover the services on Sunday, he gave me crutches and pain pills and released me for the weekend.

On Sunday afternoon I called for several friends of mine who pastored in the area and deacons of my church to gather with me and pray over the situation. I told them I wanted to preach the gospel, and I'd sure rather do it with both feet. Nevertheless, I was willing to accept God's will no matter what the outcome. I came out of that meeting with a great peace after having been anointed with oil and prayed for by these men of God. I did not know if God would spare my foot, but I did know that His will would be done.

I entered the hospital that Monday and had surgery early the next morning. I went in the operating room thinking I would never see my foot again, but I woke up in recovery still feeling my toes. I remembered the verse in the Bible about how beautiful are the feet of those who preach the gospel and thought that foot sure looked beautiful to me!

Later in the afternoon, my doctor came by to explain why he had not amputated my foot. He had routinely opened my foot to see if he could gain any valuable knowledge for future reference. When he exposed the bone, there was no break! The x-ray on the view box clearly showed the break, along with fragments of the gunpowder and evidence of previous surgeries. It was definitely the correct x-ray, but the bone had healed completely in just five days—a medical impossibility!

He called in six other doctors to verify his findings. They concluded that someone far greater than themselves was working on my foot. Two days later I walked out of the hospital.

Five years later I had severe pain and went to a specialist in Houston, Texas. After a couple of minor surgeries to relieve the pain, he referred me to Dr. Sonny Rush at the Rush Foundation Hospital in Meridian, Mississippi. After praying with me, Dr. Rush, who is also a Christian, decided rather than amputate to try a different procedure. Three weeks later I walked out of the hospital and have not had any trouble since then, except for an occasional pain that serves as a reminder of God's mercy and healing power.

Wesley Enfinger

I knew from day one that Debbie was special. I was six years old and had ordered a baby brother, but one look and I was hooked.

She always had a smile ready; but if I crossed her, those brown eyes would snap! Debbie was a normal little girl, running and playing rough with her cousins, with no problems.

She did have frequent throat infections, though, and was scheduled for a tonsillectomy before starting kindergarten. When my parents took Debbie for her preadmittance workup, the doctor on duty happened to be an orthopedic specialist. He noticed a peculiarity in her bone structure and asked if he could do a series of x-rays to check it out. The results were devastating. Debbie had a form of spina bifida. She was born with a portion of her spine missing. In fact, eight vertebrae simply weren't there, and nothing could be done about it. We were told that her prognosis was very grim and only time would tell how severe her deformity would become.

She received the Holy Ghost at a very young age and was always a witness. She was very devout about saying grace at lunchtime. What started at the beginning of first grade as, "Oh, how sweet!" soon became a situation where nobody, from the principal down, would eat lunch until Debbie was seated, had bowed her head, and asked the blessing.

As the years went by, Debbie's affliction became more noticeable. She had been anointed and prayed for many times, but God had not seen fit to heal her. Then when she was thirteen, as she stepped out of the car, her thigh bone slipped out of the hip joint. To repair this, they had to cut the bone and put in a metal plate to hold the bone together. This in turn caused the bone to stop growing. By the time Debbie had reached her full growth, one leg was two inches longer than the other. Her shoe had to be built up two inches to compensate. To accommodate this, her shoes always had to be sturdy, sensible (ugly) shoes.

Then one year at youth camp at Camp Dixie in North Carolina, things changed. O. R. Fauss preached and felt led to start a prayer line. I went back to my sister and convinced her to go through the line for prayer. She did and went back to her seat the same as before. I felt in my heart that this was Debbie's night for a miracle. I went to her and told her that if she would go through the line again God would touch her. She started to protest, and I told her, "Do it!" Something struck a cord in her, and she went back through the prayer line with determination. After prayer, she sat down on the front row.

She told God that, no matter what, she was finished with those shoes, and she kicked them off. At the end of the service as Debbie stood to her feet, she tried to compensate for the two-inch difference in her legs; however, she almost fell, for there was no two-inch difference! God had instantly added two inches to her leg. One of the ministers grabbed her shoes and marched all over the camp singing "All Hail the Power of Jesus' Name." Needless to say, we had a wonderful time rejoicing in God's goodness.

The next morning in devotion, Wayne Huntley stood and said he wanted to buy Debbie her first pair of new shoes. (She had borrowed a pair of shoes to wear to devotion.) Everyone got into the act and took up an offering to send Debbie shoe shopping.

Her healing has been a great testimony of God's goodness and power. She remains faithful to God and is the wife of a United Pentecostal pastor. They have one son, who incidentally, is another of God's miracles.

God has done so many wonderful miracles for my

immediate family: Debbie's healing, Dad's cancer healed, a brain tumor removed from me at age sixteen, Mom's rheumatoid arthritis healed, my husband's deliverance from burns received in a fire, and his subsequent return to God. The list goes on and on. I praise God for His love. He is everything to us!

Pattie Nelson

2

Provision

When I was nine, my grandmother and grand-father separated, leaving my grandmother, who was in poor health, with very little income. She had only an eighth-grade education and, except for the brief time she worked in an airplane assembly during World War II, had few work skills outside her domestic abilities.

Other than the nominal fee she received as a sitter for terminal patients, her income consisted of $140 per month and a minuscule Social Security check, which seldom covered the cost of her medication.

I watched her juggle her tiny budget, faithfully tithing and always managing to have enough to help someone in need. She told me routinely, "God will supply our needs. Maybe not all our wants, but He will supply our needs."

She also told me about faithful women in our church like Mildred Redish, who often stopped by unexpectedly with a bag of groceries at times when only God knew the cupboard was bare. I'm very thankful to all the people who were sensitive to the needs of my little Christian grandmother. She died several years ago, shortly before my daughter was born, but the lessons she taught me in our thirty-one years together have made solid places in shifting sand for me.

It is much easier to trust God for my needs when I reflect on how he supplied the needs of my grandmother. I hope I can portray this valuable lesson to my daughter, making it easier for her to trust, knowing what God has done in my life.

In her book *Prayer Takes Wings*, Thetus Tenney tells a story involving her sister Agnes, who asked her mother for a bread and jelly sandwich. Her mother told her they had neither, so Agnes climbed in their old car and prayed for bread and jelly.

A short while later, a little girl came down the lane with a sack for Agnes. The little girl said her mother was praying, and God told her to send a loaf of bread and a jar of jelly.

This story reassures me that God hears our every prayer and desires to bless us with good things. I've read the story several times to my daughter, Whitney. Now she has a story of her own!

During our back-to-school shopping recently, Whitney had in mind a particular type of lunchbox and thermos. It didn't matter that there were at least one hundred varieties of lunchboxes on the market; she wanted that one, and under no circumstance would she settle for less.

We had already been to three stores getting clothes and supplies. It seemed none of the stores had a lunchbox close to the one she wanted.

Our last stop before going home was K-Mart. It was nearly closing time, and I was exhausted from working all day, not to mention spending the past three hours in preparation for the starting school term. My instructions as we entered the store were, "This is your last chance. If you don't find one you like here, I'll make the decision for you!"

Much to our dismay, the one she wanted was nowhere in sight. As her big, brown eyes filled with tears, I told her we would pick out a backpack and then look again at lunchboxes. She could make her decision then.

Unwillingly, she walked to the next aisle with me and chose her backpack, all the while complaining because of her inability to find the lunchbox. "I really wanted that lunchbox, Mama," she said. "It makes me so mad that somebody got it!"

In my impatience I scolded, "If you want it so much, quit complaining and just pray about it!"

In utter shock she looked at me and said, "OK, I will!" And she did, right there in K-Mart, out loud!

I can't tell you how surprised I was when we went back to the other aisle and there on that near-empty shelf, in plain sight, where it definitely was not just a few seconds before, was the lunchbox of her specifications!

She wrinkled up her little nose in her "I told you so" way and said, "God put it there just for me!"

That's great if she wants to believe that, but I honestly think He put it there just for me, because I was ready to go home!

During a recent Sunday evening service Whitney sat with friends until Charlie and I came down from the choir. As we sat down for the preaching, she came to me complaining of nausea. She felt feverish, so I put her in my lap and whispered a simple prayer: "God, touch my baby now in Jesus' name. Thank You, Lord." In less than ten minutes she cooled down and went to sleep in my arms.

I noticed she had taken her shoes off and assumed she had left them where she was sitting during the early part of service. After church, I went to get them, but they were not where I had anticipated. Knowing that, even if I woke her up to ask, in her half-conscious state she would not remember where she left them, I kept on searching. After about fifteen minutes of looking in all the obvious places and realizing it would take quite a while to cover the rest of the sanctuary, checking under each pew, I simply whispered, "God, I'm tired, and I really need those shoes. Please let me find them now."

No sooner had I finished my prayer than Mariah, one of Whitney's little friends, walked up to me and said, "Whitney left her shoes on my row before church." She then directed me to where they were. I thank God that He listens to all we say and answers even our tiny little prayers.

Once while visiting her grandparents, Whitney found some rhinestones my mother had pulled off an old dress. Playing dress-up, she stuck one on her ear like an earring and dropped it into her ear canal.

I couldn't believe she had done that. I am a surgical nurse and frequently assist in removing foreign objects from the ears and noses of small children.

After several minutes of trying to remove it without trauma to her eardrum, I gave up. It appeared that we would need a special surgical instrument and microscope to remove the rhinestone. It was lodged backwards and impossible to grab with tweezers. We even tried flushing it out with water. I was, to say the least, extremely aggravated. We did not have the extra money to take her to the emergency room, which was our only choice at that time of the night.

We decided to pray. We should have done it earlier! Miraculously the stone reversed its position and was easily removed with tweezers. That little prayer spared us a lot of time and money, and kept Whitney from possibly having surgery.

From time to time we find ourselves with more month than paycheck. During these times our family is especially thankful that God supplies our needs in a number of ways I call "God's memos." I refer to them as memos because they are little reminders of His love and provision for us.

On several occasions, we have been low on food and gas money, only to search through what we knew were empty purses or suit pockets, hoping to gather change and instead finding a twenty-dollar bill. Many times I've opened my change purse to get my last few one-dollar bills and found much more than I knew I had.

On three separate occasions in the past year, we have found ten-dollar bills lying in strange places. The first was in my little girl's rocker in the living room, the second was lying neatly pressed under a sofa cushion that my husband was straightening, and the third was between the cushion and the arm of a rocking chair.

Numerous times my parents, Josh and Ouida Tucker, have given us money just because they love us and wanted to bless us, not knowing they were being used of God to supply a need.

For several years, my husband's parents, Glenn and Eunice McQuaig, owned a Western Sizzlin' Restaurant. They would often send home various cuts of meats for us to enjoy. The joke around our house was, when were broke and couldn't buy groceries, we had to eat sirloin.

It amazes me the ways in which God blesses us. Our car needed new tires, but the money for them wasn't in our month's budget. Eventually we would get them, but it would take some planning.

Around that time, we were scheduled to attend the Praise and Worship Music Gathering in Alexandria, Louisiana. Because another couple wanted to go with us, we borrowed Glenn and Eunice's van and left our car at their house. While we were away, they put new tires on our car. Glenn even washed and waxed it. Once they gave us a new washer, and they repeatedly buy Whitney new clothes (which I hope continues through her teenage years).

I pray God's continual blessings on them because they have been a blessing to us. They've taught us well about faithfulness and that we can't outgive God.

They also have shown us that many times God uses people to answer the prayers and needs of others. If we are sensitive to the Holy Ghost, we can better recognize these needs and help supply them.

Becky McQuaig

Yet setteth he the poor on high from affliction, and maketh him families like a flock (Psalm 107:41).

Fear thou not; for I am with thee: be not dismayed; for I am thy God: I will strengthen thee; yea, I will help thee; yea, I will uphold thee with the right hand of my righteousness. . . . When the poor and needy seek water, and there is none, and their tongue faileth for thirst, I the LORD will hear them. I the God of Israel will not forsake them. I will open rivers in high places, and fountains in the midst of the valley. I will make the wilderness a pool of water, and the dry land springs of water. I will plant in the wilderness the cedar, the shittah trees, and the myrtle, and the oil tree; I will set in the desert the fir tree, and the pine, and the box tree together: that they may see, and know, and consider, and understand together, that the hand of the LORD hath done this, and the Holy One of Israel hath created it (Isaiah 41:10, 17-20).

God is our refuge and strength, a very present help in trouble (Psalm 46:1).

Therefore take no thought, saying, What shall we eat? or, What shall we drink? or, Wherewithal shall we be clothed? (for after all these things do the Gentiles seek:) for your heavenly Father knoweth that ye have need of all these things (Matthew 6:31-32).

For the LORD God is a sun and shield: the LORD will give grace and glory: no good thing will he withhold from them that walk uprightly (Psalm 84:11).

Trust in the LORD, and do good; so shalt thou dwell in the land, and verily thou shalt be fed (Psalm 37:3).

He maketh peace in thy borders and filleth thee with the finest of the wheat (Psalm 147:14).

My wife and I were preaching in Mississippi, back when we first started out, and we ran out of gas on an old gravel road. We had ten cents between us and spent that on gas, but it wasn't enough to get our old truck going.

I prayed for help, and the Lord sent a fellow who had a full tank of gas. I told him I was a preacher and was trying to get a certain place. The man put a siphon hose from his tank to mine and got the truck running. Then he just kept on letting it run in my tank.

I told him it was enough, but he said he could get more and kept right on. He gave me plenty to get me where I was going.

D. L. Welch

He hath given meat unto them that fear him: he will ever be mindful of his covenant (Psalm 111:5).

But my God shall supply all your need according to his riches in glory by Christ Jesus (Philippians 4:19).

I will abundantly bless her provision: I will satisfy her poor with bread (Psalm 132:15).

Though ye have lien among the pots, yet shall ye be as the wings of a dove covered with silver, and her feathers with yellow gold (Psalm 68:13).

He will regard the prayer of the destitute, and not despise their prayer (Psalm 102:17).

The righteous cry, and the Lord *heareth, and delivereth them out of all their troubles* (Psalm 34:17).

And I will send grass in the fields for thy cattle, that thou mayest eat and be full (Deuteronomy 11:15).

A couple of years ago I registered my dog with a

breeding service. Within a few days, I met with an interested couple and received a check for $115.

Early the next morning, a lady I know called me with a specific need of $100. She told me she was praying for God to fill the need and felt that He told her to call me.

I knew immediately that God had given me the money for this purpose. I am thankful and privileged that He allowed me the opportunity to help a friend in need.

Ben Goodson

So many times, when we think of God's provisions for us, we think of them in a physical or material sense. Too often, we forget His spiritual provisions.

All of us, in our walk with God, have gone through dry places, times when we were weary and our strength was gone. But just as God provides for us in the natural, He also supplies our spiritual needs.

I have been enlightened to a great truth: If I do not walk through the valleys, I will not appreciate the beauty of the mountaintop. If I see no darkness, I will not comprehend the wonder of the light. If I am never weary, I cannot tell others of God's refreshing. If I am never afraid, I will not know the strength of His protecting hand. If there is never a need, I will not understand the grace of God. If I am never tempted, I will not know that He has made a way of escape.

Becky McQuaig

I have made you and I will carry you; I will sustain you and I will rescue you (Isaiah 46:2, NIV).

My grace is sufficient for thee: for my strength is made perfect in weakness (II Corinthians 12:9).

Surely he shall deliver thee from the snare of the fowler, and from the noisome pestilence. . . . Because he hath set his love upon me, therefore will I deliver him: I will set him on high, because he hath known my name. He shall call upon me, and I will answer him: I will be with him in trouble; I will deliver him, and honour him (Psalm 91:3, 14-15).

The LORD will give strength unto his people; the LORD will bless his people with peace (Psalm 29:11).

The LORD is my light and my salvation; whom shall I fear? the LORD is the strength of my life; of whom shall I be afraid? (Psalm 27:1).

The LORD is my shepherd; I shall not want. He maketh me to lie down in green pastures: he leadeth me beside the still waters. He restoreth my soul: he leadeth me in the paths of righteousness for his name's sake. Yea, though I walk through the valley of the shadow of death, I will fear no evil: for thou art with me; thy rod and thy staff they comfort me. Thou preparest a table before me in the presence of mine enemies: thou anointest my head with oil; my cup runneth over. Surely goodness and mercy shall follow me all the days of my life: and I will dwell in the house of the LORD for ever (Psalm 23).

For he satisfieth the longing soul, and filleth the hungry soul with goodness (Psalm 107:9).

There hath no temptation taken you but such as is common to man: but God is faithful, who will not suffer you to be tempted above that ye are able; but will with the temptation also make a way to escape, that ye may be able to bear it (I Corinthians 10:13).

3

Protection

rotection is one aspect in which God is frequently apparent in our lives. We must believe the Bible when it says, "The steps of a good man are ordered by the LORD" (Psalm 37:23), and, "O LORD, I know that the way of man is not in himself: it is not in man that walketh to direct his steps" (Jeremiah 10:23).

God is in control! Whatever happens to us, whether it be good or bad, is either ordered or allowed by God. He permits what we see as misfortune or calamities so that we can achieve spiritual growth and maturity. Adversity has a way of breaking our own will so that we will accept His will. It brings us to our knees, where we find strength and comfort. What we may see as a curse can actually be a blessing in disguise.

It is difficult for us to believe that God is interested and involved in every detail of our existence, but Matthew 10:29-31 says: "Are not two sparrows sold for a farthing? and one of them shall not fall on the ground without your Father. But the very hairs of your head are all numbered. Fear ye not therefore, ye are of more value than many sparrows." We do not know the exact amount of divine intervention that takes place on our behalf, but undoubtedly it is astronomical!

Only when we view problems in the spiritual realm can we understand what is taking place. When the servant of Elijah had his eyes opened in a spiritual sense, he could see the heavenly host encamped about them for protection. They were completely surrounded by an angelic army poised for combat, but God had provided their defense.

God has not changed. The Bible teaches that He is the same yesterday, today, and forever. Just as He allowed the enemy to surround Elijah and His servant, so He may allow misfortune to enter our lives, but He is ever in control!

One day while cutting a fallen tree into small pieces to use for firewood, I suffered a severe injury. The chainsaw kicked back, forcing the running blade into my face. Though bleeding profusely and in pain, I felt peace come over me and knew that God was with me.

Having been brought up in a Christian home, I understood that bad things do happen to good people. God was not punishing me. Instead I felt that God had confidence in me that I would keep my faith even through adversity.

The injury was severe, and I suffered the loss of several teeth. My lip and chin were cut through, exposing my jawbone. My wife, Becky, is a surgical nurse and knew exactly what to do. She and Whitney were dressed, ready to walk out the door to go shopping, when I was injured. Had I been cut just a few minutes later than I was, I would have been home alone with no one to help me.

Because of the force of the blow, I was dazed and assumed I had only knocked out a few teeth. All the while I thought I had been hit with the back end of the chainsaw and not the blade! It took only the look on Becky's face to let me know otherwise.

Grabbing towels to hold pressure, she notified the emergency room of my status and pending arrival. We lived about five minutes from the hospital, but "Air Becky" got me there in less than three.

Whitney rode in the back seat with her little hand on my shoulder, praying. I'm not sure if she was praying for me or her mother's driving, but nonetheless she prayed!

The evidence of God's protection was undeniable! The blade had missed the facial nerve by half an inch. It had also missed my carotid artery by half an inch. Had my artery been severed, I would have bled to death in a couple of minutes. The doctor commented that if I had to choose the best place on the face to have such an injury, the area injured was exactly the correct place!

The only permanent damage was numbness to a portion of my lip and a large scar down the front of my chin. I consider it to be a reminder of God's protection. I believe that God allowed this experience but controlled the outcome from the beginning.

God's protection sometimes entails prevention, but often He chooses simply to sustain and strengthen. He will not leave us alone. He will stay close beside us.

Charles McQuaig

When I was about eleven, we received a phone call one morning before dawn. My grandmother's next-door neighbor was calling to tell my parents that Granny's house was on fire. She said Granny had been rescued, but she did not know how severe her injuries were.

My grandmother lived alone and had a substantial hearing loss. Apparently she had not heard the crackling of the flames or the collapse of burning rafters. Much of her little house was consumed.

The miracle is that her neighbor had awakened early that morning and started her housework. As she took her rugs out to shake them on the back porch, she noticed smoke billowing from the roof. Screaming for her husband's help, she ran to call the fire department. He rushed to Granny's bedroom window. My grandmother was a portly woman, considerably heavier than he, but by the grace of God he managed to pull her through the window to safety.

Granny had a habit of opening the window by her

bed about two inches every night so she could breathe fresh air while she slept. Concerned for her safety, we cautioned her frequently about that practice, fearing it would facilitate easy access to someone trying to burglarize her home. The fire chief said she might have died from smoke inhalation had she not been near that open window. It also kept her neighbor from having to break out the window in order to open it, which probably would have caused him to be too late, considering the progression of the fire.

She managed to escape with only wounded pride and a scorched nightgown. Otherwise, she had no significant injuries from the blaze.

Thanks be to God for His early morning wake-up calls and placing people at the right place at the right time!

On one of our visits with Charlie's sister, Sherry, and her husband, Doug, in Greenville, South Carolina, our daughter, Whitney, was playing outside on the driveway. Suddenly she dashed in the house to get her doll. Less than two minutes after her abrupt entry, Doug came in saying he had just killed a four-foot snake in the exact spot she had been playing. I'm glad God put thoughts in her mind to run get her doll.

When Whitney was three, we lived in a two-story house. One afternoon I sat down at the top of the stairs to talk to my sister, Pam, who lived with us at the time. She was standing on the landing in front of me. Whitney came up from behind to hug me and turned to play in the hall.

In an instant she stepped through the rails of the banister. I only caught a glimpse of her out of my peripheral vision, but reflex caused me to grab her shirt without realizing what I had done.

Her body would have easily made it through the rails, but I doubt if her head would have. She would have either fallen to the hard tile below or broken her neck. Thank God for putting me there to catch her!

I work at a large medical complex that has an employee parking area across the highway. I was cutting it a little close as far as getting to work on time and decided I had better walk across to the building rather than wait for the shuttle.

I punched the button at the intersection that causes the traffic light to change and gives the signal to cross. As the signal came on, I started off the sidewalk, but for some reason hesitated. Just moments later, a car ran the red light. The driver obviously did not see the light, because he didn't even slow down.

Had I not hesitated, I would have been his new hood ornament. I'm confident it was God's protecting hand that held me back those few life-saving seconds.

Our family has a little getaway house on a lake about forty miles from where we live. On one visit there, I was munching on some popcorn when a tiny piece went down the wrong pipe, causing a vocal cord spasm and a total air lock. Unable to call for help, I stood there beating myself in the chest and flailing my arms for at least a solid minute before I could capture anyone's attention.

Finally, Charlie, seeing my predicament, began the Heimlich maneuver. After several attempts, the only thing he accomplished was the bruising of my ribs.

I was getting dizzy and very weak from the lack of oxygen. He tried again, at which time I was able to inhale a very small breath, but again I could not exhale.

I ran into the kitchen, not wanting my child to see me choke to death. Charlie followed me and with desperation in his voice cried out, "In Jesus' name!"

At that instant, as if someone had pulled the stopper in a drain, I felt an immediate release in my throat. Oxygen was never more appreciated than at that moment. I had been without air for roughly two and a half minutes and no doubt would not have survived much longer.

I realized through that incident that all my efforts and actions are in vain without Jesus! In my panic, I tried to do it all my way, which obviously is the carnal nature of man, but when my efforts failed, the utterance of the name of Jesus reminded my spirit that God is in control of our circumstances and that whatever we ask in His name, He will do it. (See John 14:13-14.)

Becky McQuaig

Recently, during a sudden storm, the wind and rain began pelting against my youngest child's window. I ran in his room when I heard the unusual noise, pulled Michael away from the window, and began to pray.

The storm subsided immediately, and only the sound of the rain on the roof prevailed.

That evening as we were leaving to go to church, we noticed that a very large tree limb had fallen and was lying on top of the hedges, right under the window to Michael's room. I then realized how close we had come to being hurt during the storm. Had the limb been thrown through the window, either Michael or both of us would have suffered serious injury.

Surely God protected us. He is so wonderful!

Marie Bush

While delivering a heavy, beveled-glass top for a coffee table one afternoon, my foot slipped off the back of the truck. I fell over four feet to the hard pavement, landing flat on my back. The glass top, which had slipped out of my hands, fell against the back of the truck and broke into several sharp, jagged pieces. They came crashing down on me, severely lacerating my forehead and left brow.

Bleeding profusely and somewhat disoriented, I called for help. No one could hear me, so I desperately tried to get to my feet. Weakened and unable to see through the blood, I managed to get to the door of the house where I was making the delivery.

The customer's teenage daughter came to the door and screamed, "Oh my God, somebody help!"

I figured by her reaction that I must have been cut badly.

The emergency room doctor said the glass had punctured an artery in my forehead. If it had been just one-half inch lower it would have gone directly into my left eye.

Every morning when I see the scar that extends from my hairline to my brow, I have to say, "Thank You, God, that I still have eyes to see it!"

Ben Goodson

When I was a young woman I lived in a rental house alone. The day I moved out, another young woman moved in. That night the house was broken into and she was assaulted. The man who did this was later found and arrested. It was suspected that he had been stalking the house.

I am very sorry for the unfortunate incident the young woman went through, and I hope the emotional scars have healed. At the same time, I am very grateful for God's protection, because I know the assault was intended for me!

Ouida Tucker
(Becky McQuaig's mother)

In 1952, I worked the night shift at St. Regis Paper Company. I had seven children, the baby being eight months old. When he wanted me for anything, he would say, "Mommy, Mommy, Mommy." He would not say it just one time but always three or more times, even when I answered him the first time. One day this practice had really gotten on my nerves, and I tried to explain that he needed to call only once.

That night I left home at 10:30 to go to work. The next morning, about 7:15, I was on my way home. Having not had much sleep in the last few days, I fell asleep at the wheel. I have no idea how fast I was driving, but the voice of my baby cried out, "Mommy, Mommy, Mommy!" I awoke out of my sleep and found myself on the wrong side of the road approaching a sharp curve. I immediately changed lanes and slowed down, thus avoiding the impending wreck. I will always give God the glory for saving my life through the voice of my baby.

Lottie Ezell Davis

We lived in an old house on Pensacola Bay with driveway access to the front and back of the house. Every school day at 3:00 I picked up my daughter at school. This particular day, I chose to park in the front yard. As I pulled up to the house, I saw that the front double doors were wide open. My first thought was that the wind had blown them open, and I wondered if I had forgotten to lock them.

We had been warned that when people live on the water, if they get burglarized it is from the water side. I had heard that the best protection for a home is a big dog in the yard and a small one in the house. For protection, my daughter, Rachel, and I had been to the city pound and found a lhasa-apso that we both had fallen in love with.

From outward appearances my world was falling apart. Newly divorced, with one son off to college and the second son living with his father, I had a nine-year-old daughter to raise alone. We were left in a big house (over five thousand square feet) with huge windows, the bottom portion being solid pieces of glass. Needless to say, it was impossible to "burglar proof."

The house was virtually impossible to sell because of financial problems from the marriage. My future seemed to be locked up in court waiting for the sale. In the meantime, Rachel and I were attempting to survive on very little income.

I offered the boys' room to Sonja, a single girl in our church. She accepted the offer, and now Rachel felt as if she had a big sister. Sonja quickly became part of the family, and the boys' room became a home for her. She kept a hope chest at the foot of her bed with sterling silver flatware on the bottom, neatly covered with blankets.

On this day, when I saw the opened doors, my fear was not that the house was burglarized but that the little dog was gone. As Rachel got her books together in the car, I ran inside searching for the dog. As I came in, the dog ran out from Sonja's room. Relieved, I turned and walked into my bedroom, only to find it turned up side down. Every drawer had been pulled out and thrown all over the room.

Fear gripped me. My daughter was coming inside, and there might be burglars still in the house. At the same time, she came running in, asking, "Mama, what were those two men doing running across the back yard?"

I grabbed her and ran next door to the neighbor's house. We called the police, and for the next hour they searched the house, attic, garage, and every inch of the yard. I wanted to be sure that no one else was still in hiding.

Three hours later, I found myself standing in the yard watering my half-dead roses. I was numb, and somehow watering the flowers seemed like a kind of therapy. Rachel and her little dog were soon back to normal, but I could only thank God and struggle to trust Him no matter what our uncertain future held.

About 5:00 P.M. Sonja pulled up. I called her over and said, "I have some good news and some bad news. First, I don't think they got anything, but we've been hit, and your room is turned upside down; even the mattress is leaning against the fireplace!"

Sonja's face went snow white. I quickly tried to comfort her. "I really don't think they got anything. Rachel saw them, and they weren't carrying anything. They had opened your hope chest, but they had one more blanket to go before reaching your sterling silver."

She interrupted me, "Jo, you don't understand: Now I understand last night! At 3:00 A.M. I woke up with a sentence going over and over in my mind: Get your gun out from under your mattress and put it in the top shelf of your closet!

"I got so mad at myself. I needed my rest so bad, and all I could do was think of one sentence over and over and over. After thirty minutes I threw back my covers and told myself I might as well get up and do it if I wanted to get some sleep! Jo, what if I had not done it? They would have found my gun right when you were walking into the house. That was God!"

A peace swept over me. Sonja later had to move away, and our outside dog died. Rachel and I lived in the house alone for another year, but we were never afraid, because we knew God would always take care of us.

Jo Bailey

About four or five years ago we stopped at a gas station for fuel. It was not raining, but as I stepped out to fill the tank, a bolt of lightning struck the pump, went through me, and knocked me against the car.

I was taken to the hospital and kept overnight to see if there was any damage. There was no damage! The Lord had been with me and provided the protection I needed.

Ralph Reid

I was tired of being pregnant and miserable from staying in doors, so my husband, Josh, and I decided to go for a boat ride in Escambia Bay. When we got to the middle of the bay, the motor went dead. Josh tried unsuccessfully to start it again. It was late July and very hot. Even with the heat, I was relatively calm until a midsummer thunderstorm came along.

Josh tried his best to paddle the boat to shore and outrun the impending storm, but he wasn't fast enough. Lightning was popping all around, and I became very frightened. Within a few minutes I began having contractions!

You can believe I started praying!

We made it to shore, but we were far from where we launched. A very nice man spotted us, invited us into his home, and later took us back to our car.

Thankfully the pains subsided for the moment, but only a few days later I gave birth to a precious, five-pound baby girl.

I'm so glad God protected my baby and me.

Otherwise she would never have grown up to be the co-author of this book.

Ouida Tucker

One Sunday afternoon almost nine years ago, I was on my way to church around 5:15 in the evening. Suddenly, I saw a car heading straight for me!

Traffic was extremely heavy with cars in all four lanes. When I saw the car cross the yellow line just five hundred feet ahead of me, I knew I had nowhere to go to avoid an accident. Putting on my brakes, I realized that I might die in a matter of seconds! I felt totally helpless. All I remember doing was yelling out loud, "Jesus, help me!"

No sooner were the words out of my mouth than it was as if a huge hand reached down and picked up cars, moving them so that the oncoming car could get out of my way. I saw cars move directly sideways, which is physically impossible!

The only damage was caused by a big station wagon that hit a small brick wall, knocking it down. The station wagon wasn't even damaged!

When all the cars were stopped and out of the way, I went back to see if the person in the station wagon was injured. As I reached his car, he looked at me and said, "Lady, someone upstairs was looking out for you today!" I could only agree!

The car that crossed the yellow line was driven by a young girl who had just received her driver's license and new car that day. She was heading to the Pizza Hut to meet her parents and thought she had entered a turning lane, not realizing there wasn't one. She was sorry and very shaken up.

I got into my car and praised the Lord all the way to church. I knew the Lord had rescued me and had given me the gift of life for a while longer.

Lois Waldman

There are times when we need an immediate response from God, when we don't have time to pray and fast, when we can't get on our knees, repent, worship, and then make our request known. There are situations when we have barely enough time to call out the name of Jesus, but what an awesome power is in that name! This is a testimony about such a time.

My husband and I were staying in a hotel awaiting our return to the United States after a three-year tour in Spain. It was close to midnight on the last night of our stay, and we had just returned from a farewell dinner at a friend's house. My husband went down to the lobby for a minute. Both of us were excited about the trip home. We still had some last-minute packing to do, so neither of us planned to sleep.

While he was gone, I heard the door open. I

turned in time to see my dog run into the hallway, with the door quickly closing behind her. Wondering what was going on, I followed. To my surprise, when I opened the door I found a large man there. He seemed confused and surprised himself. I sensed no danger and thought he perhaps had the wrong room.

My dog excitedly jumped all around the two of us. The man seemed afraid. I tried to comfort him and reassure him that she would not bite, that she was just very playful. He then bent down to play with her. Looking back on this incident, I realize he was just positioning himself to ease his way into the doorway. When I reached down to pick up the dog, he would not let go of her. I noticed the obvious smell of alcohol on his breath.

In one sweeping motion, he released her, stood up, stepped into my room, and closed the door. I saw the look on his face change from boyish confusion to vicious intent. I knew he was going to hurt me, and there was no way I could do anything to stop him!

As he came toward me, I stepped back and cried, "Oh, Jesus." I screamed, "What are you doing in my room?" He didn't answer but kept coming toward me. I quickly backed out of the room through the sliding glass doors and against the balcony gate. I could go no further. Terrified, I started screaming louder than I thought I could scream.

He continued to come toward me until he was about eight feet away. Suddenly he stopped! His entire countenance changed. He looked at me as if to say,

"Where am I, what am I doing here?" Then he turned and walked out of the room and into the hall, closing the door behind him. I stood on the balcony stunned!

I don't know if he saw something that made him stop, or if God just caused him to change his mind. I don't know how God did it, but I do know He handled the situation.

Jessica N. Isaacs

I was on my way to school one rainy morning, running late, and thus I was traveling a little too fast. As I reached for my purse, the car began to hydroplane. I hit a large rock, and my head crashed into the windshield. I barely avoided hitting a tree, stopping only inches away.

When the police arrived, they said I would have probably been killed had I hit the tree. A witness commented that it looked as if a large hand kept my head from going through the windshield, cushioning the blow and protecting me. I know God kept me from being severely injured.

Melissa Baker

Looking back over the past ten years of my life, I

realize just how valuable the prayers of my immediate family and church family have been. Their prayers, and God's divine purpose for me, are the only reasons that I am still here. I would like to share a few life-and-death experiences for the glory of God.

I was raised in the Christian faith. After a traumatic divorce from twelve years of marriage, I quit going to church. I fell into a deep state of depression, during which time God continually kept His hand on me.

On two occasions, I had suicidal tendencies. I wanted to escape. Nevertheless, God was there to rescue me from myself.

I started drinking a lot and often did not remember driving home. Sometimes I didn't make it home. One time, I passed out in an ant bed. I woke up to see my legs looking like those of person suffering from elephantiasis. They had been eaten by hundreds of ants. The emergency room doctor had never seen anything like it and told me my legs would probably never be normal again. I wore pants for six months to hide all the hideous scars. I am fortunate the ants didn't get to my face.

Another time, after I left a nightclub, the brakes went out on my car and caused the car to flip over. Yet another night my car rolled several times as I came off the interstate highway, and it landed on the driver's side. Most of the glass in the car was broken, but I did not have a scratch! What makes it even more miraculous was that I wasn't wearing my seatbelt! I felt reassurance when the ambulance driver turned out to be a

Pentecostal minister, for I had been raised in a Pentecostal church.

Once, a cab driver spotted me leaning over on the steering wheel of my car while I was driving across the Pensacola Bay Bridge. This was one of the many times God was my pilot!

I was struck by lightning in 1993 and sustained no injuries. I believe God has kept me around for a special purpose, even through all my stupidity.

The greatest miracle of all happened in June 1994 during a singles conference in Pensacola, Florida, in which Lee Stoneking was a guest speaker. Hands that knew how, picked up all my broken pieces, put them back on the potter's wheel, and made me a new vessel. God forgave me of my terrible past, delivered me from alcohol and drugs, and is continuously healing my mind!

Jackie Holbrook

God protects and blesses me daily. Because of a physical problem, I am unable to get a driver's license, and I frequently rely on hitchhiking for my transportation needs. I have done this since I was sixteen years of age.

I always pray, "Lord, please provide me with a safe ride to my destination. I put my life in Your hands, and in Jesus' name I ask this." Then I stick out my thumb, and God always supplies a ride. I have faith that God will provide my needs if I ask in His name.

Once, while riding my bicycle, I was hit by a truck. The only injuries I sustained were bruises on my leg. God protected me and let me live. He even blessed me with a new bike!

Sunshine Domini

On Christmas Eve, 1970, my husband and I were on our way to the hospital to check on our daughter, Jackie, who had surgery to remove some embedded wisdom teeth. We were traveling down the outside lane when a man in a Cadillac drove by us in the inside lane at a very high rate of speed.

It had been raining, and the pavement was wet at the time. Without any signal, he turned directly in front of our car. As I saw what was happening I cried, "Jesus." It seemed as if an angel stopped our car on a dime.

The man in the Cadillac was drunk and had passed out at the wheel. His car made three complete spins in front of us and hit a telephone pole. His car was so close to us that when he crashed, his battery acid sprayed across the hood of our car.

I know God intervened for us that day because our cars never made contact with each other. Psalm 46:1 says, "God is our refuge and strength, a very present help in trouble."

Rachel Daughtry

On Labor Day, September 1, 1975, my brother and I went swimming in Blackwater River. I dove into the water headfirst, as I had done so many times before. This time, however, my head hit bottom, breaking my neck and paralyzing me.

Though unable to move, I somehow floated to the surface. My brother, Keith, pulled me to the shore, where two men helped him load me on the back of the truck. Keith, who was only fourteen at the time, drove me to the hospital.

Miraculously, on the way to the hospital I regained feeling and could move again. By the time I was x-rayed, I had been moved five times without the aid of a board or cervical stabilization.

X-rays revealed a C-5 fracture so severely separated that the doctor said he could see daylight through the break.

I spent twenty-seven days in traction and finally had surgery. A bone graft was taken from my hip to fuse my cervical vertebrae. I still have two screws in place from the surgery, I guess to keep my head on straight.

I know how blessed I am. I could easily have been killed or remained paralyzed and confined to a wheelchair for the rest of my life. Instead, I am a walking testimony of God's protecting, healing hand.

I'm grateful for His loving mercy on my life and

thankful to be able to proclaim His truth wherever I go.

Wayne Hinote

My daughter and I were traveling down the road in our car, and I needed to switch lanes. Looking back and seeing no problem, I started to change lanes.

Robin and I both felt the car slide sideways, back into the lane we had just come from. I had not turned the wheel. It was an outside force!

Just as we were pushed back in the first lane, a car that had been in my blind spot passed by. I'm thankful for the hand of God, which gently pushed us to safety and protected our lives.

Lola Richardson

4

Angelic Visitation

While driving to work on Interstate Highway 10 one beautiful spring day, I reviewed my less than perfect morning and prayed that the rest of my day would follow a different course.

Little had gone well that morning. I was frustrated and feeling guilty over my lack of self-control as I encountered my daughter's failure to gather her things for school, tie her shoes, and get in the car in a timely fashion. As rushed as most mornings are, this one seemed to be particularly hurried. I begged God to forgive my bad attitude and give me a heavy dose of much-needed patience.

I had noticed earlier how clear and blue the sky was except for a few scattered clouds in the distance. Suddenly, before my eyes, an extremely low-hanging cloud appeared just ahead. I watched in amazement as the cloud took the shape of a perfectly formed, enormous winged angel.

My verbal response was simply, "Wow, God, how neat!" I believe this cloud was a reminder from God of His tremendous love for me, even when everything seems to be going wrong. As I passed beneath the cloud, I was reminded that God is ever with me and has angels fighting my battles for me. They are not cute, little fairy-tale creatures but fierce, mighty warriors. I felt great confidence and security knowing that if God took the time to form a cloud just for my reassurance, I surely would not encounter a problem in my day that He couldn't handle.

Checking in my mirror to catch one last glimpse as I passed under it, I found the cloud had disappeared as quickly as it had come.

During a visit with my husband's sister and brother-in-law in Greenville, South Carolina, I tucked my little girl into bed and lay beside her to enjoy our snuggle time and prayer. As she drifted off to sleep, I felt a tremendous unsettling come over me. I found myself in intercessory prayer over the soul of this young child.

I knew that Satan desired to destroy her. I felt an unholy presence in the room. My physical strength drained from my body. Calling desperately on the name of Jesus for help, I fell into an unnatural sleep.

I don't remember dreaming anything, but my husband began calling my name. As I awoke, he was standing over me with a look of panic on his face. He said he had tried to wake me for nearly ten minutes, and he was getting ready to call for help when I opened my eyes.

I transferred to the other room and crawled into my bed feeling totally drained. A street light just outside the room made it seem like dawn inside. On previous nights it had been difficult to sleep, but this night I had no trouble.

Sometime during the night, I was awakened by what sounded like the flap of wings. When I opened my eyes I saw, hovering over me, the most foul, gruesome creature I had ever encountered.

I was paralyzed with fear. I tried to reach over to Charlie, but the pressure was so strong that I could not get anything to move. I knew it was a demonic spirit, but I also knew that the name of Jesus would deliver me. Though I could not speak, I began to pray, calling on Jesus.

A voice in my mind said, "Look to the light. Look to the light." The only things I could move were my eyes. As I looked toward the window where the street light was shining, a huge, winged creature in sparkling white appeared and devoured the hideous being.

The room was illuminated with the presence of this holy figure. My paralysis left, and I moved my hand toward Charlie. As I whispered, "Jesus," my fear left, and a peace like I had never experienced came over me. There was no longer any need to wake my husband, so I turned over and went back to sleep, knowing that God had sent an angel to fight the battle.

When my daughter, Whitney, was about three years old, I noticed her one afternoon as she played on her swing. She appeared to be talking with someone. I frantically opened the back door, thinking a stranger had entered the yard and was in a position unseen through the window.

When I found her alone, I asked her with whom she had been talking. Without hesitation, she replied, "My angel." I asked if she really saw someone and she emphatically said, "Yes, Mommy, he was sitting on the monkey bars"! I asked her what the angel looked like, and she said, "He's big!" I asked if she was afraid, and she just said, "No, he's nice."

I wonder if God allowed her to see her guardian angel!

Becky McQuaig

Due to the gun-related death of a neighbor's child, we decided to sell our gun. A man called in response to our newspaper advertisement, and I supplied him with our address so that he could look at the gun.

When I opened the door, he tried to push his way inside. I told him I would meet him outside and shut the door.

As the man looked at the gun, I became uneasy. I began to question him on his purpose for purchasing a gun. When I asked if he was a policeman he replied, "No. Why do you ask?"

Immediately, I told him that a policeman was on his way to look at the gun. As soon as I said it, I started to repent in my heart for lying, for I had no knowledge of a policeman's coming. While asking God's forgiveness, I heard a small voice say, "You didn't say that, I did!"

When I looked up, there was a police car at the street corner by my house. When I pointed out to the man that the policeman had come, he immediately shoved the gun into my hand and took off in his truck.

The policeman nodded at me and continued down the street. I called my neighbor and asked her to stop the policeman who was coming toward her house. She and I were both on portable phones, so she ran outside to stop him.

He was nowhere to be found! He seemed to vanish. He must have been an angel, because there is only one way out of my neighborhood. I was shaken up by the incident but immediately began to praise God, because I knew without a doubt that He was watching over me.

I went into the office to put my phone down and noticed that the answer machine was blinking. It had recorded the whole conversation between this man and me. Here was another reminder that God was in control. For the answering machine to record, a call has to come in, but I had the phone outside with me the whole time the man was looking at the gun.

Now I can honestly say that I have met a cop who is an angel!

Becky Myers

One day in Ft. Worth, Texas, my daughter and I were at home and had turned on a burner to heat up grease to fry French fries. I walked out of the kitchen briefly and became sidetracked, completely forgetting the grease on the stove.

I caught a glimpse of a man in white clothing walking into my kitchen. I felt shock, yet a curious feeling came over me. I followed the man into the kitchen only to find the pan of grease on the verge of bursting into flames. The man in white was nowhere to be found!

I feel sure it was an angel helping me to avoid a fire.

Marie Bush

Several years ago, I was on my way home from Caryville, Florida, where I was visiting with relatives. I had made this trip numerous times before.

I had often wondered what I'd do if I had a flat tire on the interstate highway. I had never changed a tire before, but had seen it done a few times. As it happened, this was the time I found out.

Traveling west on Interstate 10, I noticed a strange noise coming from my car. I pulled over to the side of the road and discovered that my right rear tire was flat. I looked both ways up the interstate. One car was heading east, there was no exit in sight, and no cars were coming on my side of the interstate.

Here goes nothing, I thought to myself. I opened my trunk and removed my bicycle, intending to place it in the back seat. As I walked around the side of the car, I looked both ways again—still no cars in sight. After placing the bicycle on the seat of the car, I noticed that a white pick-up truck had pulled up behind me. I was surprised because only seconds before there had been no cars.

A tall, muscular young man stepped out of the truck. He was wearing a white T-shirt and white pants. After graciously offering his help, he changed my tire for me.

I told him, "Thank you. I really appreciate your help."

He got in his truck. I started my car and pulled onto the interstate, and he pulled out after me. I looked through my side mirrors and he was right behind me. I looked again from the inside mirror and he was still behind me. However, the third time I looked, I did not see him at all! Thinking he may have pulled into the other lane to pass me, I looked for his car. It was not there!

There were no exits, and he had not pulled off the

road. Turning around and looking out the rear window, I could see that he had not crossed the median.

Just as quickly as he appeared, he had disappeared! All I can say is, "Thank You, Lord, for that tire-changing angel."

Sue Woodson

One night as I slept, I had a dream in which my spirit came out of my body. In the dream, I looked down at myself and thought, Well, I'll be; there I am sleeping.

Then I felt as if I were in heaven. I saw a very large choir of angels singing. They were dressed in white robes, whiter than anyone can imagine. The robes were like the sun shining behind a cloud, extremely bright, and without spot or wrinkle. The choir was singing a song I had never heard before. I would title it "The Love of God," for it was filled to capacity with love. It wasn't words that communicated the love but rather the perfect harmony. The song was beautiful!

As the angels sang, I noticed two angels standing by themselves. I asked them, "Where can I find Jesus?" I seemed to speak without opening my mouth. The two angels moved, and I saw a holy figure standing there. My eyes were fastened on Him.

I fell on my knees and bowed my face to the ground. The love that radiated from Jesus let me know for the first time how He could go the cross for my sins. He reached out His right hand to me, placed His left hand over my head, and said, "Serve Me." I was filled with love and responded, "Don't let me leave this place!" He again said, "Serve me." Through this thrilling experience, I have been able to witness to and lead several people to the Lord.

Lucille Blackwell

One night my best friend, Kim, and I were talking about the trials we were going through and how we were struggling. It must have been about 5:30 A.M. when we finally went to bed.

About ten minutes after we turned the lights out, the bedroom door opened and someone walked in. A shadow fell over me, frightening me, so I pulled the covers over my head.

Kim asked, "Charla, did you get up?"

I replied, "No."

She then said, "Someone just walked in here in a long, white robe, looked over us, and walked out."

I asked, "Kim, can you believe that God sent one of His angels to check on us?"

Later in the morning, we got up and asked her mom and her sister if either of them had come into our room. They told us they had not and that neither of them had been wearing white!

Charla White

I was driving in southern Louisiana along a bayou, late at night on my way to work. I became very sleepy and started to doze while driving. Suddenly, something white appeared in front of my car.

It was like putting my finger in a light socket! I was awake and aware of a presence. I was definitely awake the rest of the journey! I believe God sent an angel to keep me out of the bayou.

Darvin D. Kobold

I was awakened one night by a strange sensation. I felt as if someone was going to harm me. I had felt that way before and just decided that it must simply be paranoia. I tried to go back to sleep. Again, only minutes later, I felt fear. I got out of bed to get some water. As I was returning to bed, I felt it again as I passed the front door.

Being determined and stubborn, I thought I'd just dismiss it as an overactive imagination. As I stood there struggling in my mind, the Holy Ghost said simply: "Danger. Pray." The message was unmistakable. Immediately I began to pray.

God has not given us a spirit of fear but of power, love, and a sound mind so I claimed this promise and asked Him in Jesus' name to protect me with His angels. At the word "angels," I became aware of another realm. This awareness was so awesome that I cannot fully describe it. Hundreds of angels were worshiping and praising God. Their single-mindedness was incredible.

Above their thundering praise I could hear a voice. Although I couldn't make out each word clearly, I knew it was spoken on my behalf. Something greater was happening than what I was able to understand. As I looked around me, I realized that there were not just a few hundred, but thousands of angels, and they kept appearing before me, praising and worshiping God. I did the only reasonable thing to do: I joined them in worship.

At the time I didn't realize it, but there was more going on than someone trying to harm me. I didn't know what was going on, but I did know that angels were on the scene to protect me.

As quickly as the vision came, it left. I found myself on the floor. I collected my thoughts and started back to bed. In the corner of my eye, I saw the front door standing wide open. I distinctly remember locking the door and rechecking the deadbolt before going to bed. Now it was open!

I wondered to myself how long it had been open so I looked at the clock. It was 4:00 AM. Four hours had passed since I had awakened. What seemed like moments had been hours.

Although the vision had gone, I knew God's angels were still around. Calmly, I approached the door, closed it again, locked it, returned to bed, and slept till noon. His angels were watching over me, and no harm would befall me. I was reassured that He would cause all things to work together for my good. God knew what He was doing. He knew what tomorrow would hold. His angels were there to help complete His plan for me. I had nothing to worry about.

This was not the only time I have seen angels. Many times I have seen them during church services. One night I saw an angel perched on the ledge of the balcony watching us intensely, seemingly awestruck at our worship. At other times I have seen angels among people praying at the altar, again watching intently. And other times they have been engaged in battle.

Angels are always around us, but it is not the presence of angels that makes me quiver. It is the presence and power of God.

Kasondra Kent

I once saw five angels. One of them was particularly outstanding, for I witnessed as he fought against a demon and overcame him.

Another time, I was very ill and in the hospital. Two angels stood by my bed, one on either side. I could see them clearly. They were iridescent. I tried to tell them how beautiful they were, but they didn't want to hear that.

Betty Manson

While cleaning the Sunday school rooms in the old auditorium of the church one afternoon, I saw two men walk down the hall. When I went to see where they had gone, I couldn't find them. I knew that no one was supposed to be there at that time, especially strangers.

Minutes later, D. L. Welch came in. I told him what had happened and asked if he had seen anyone. He had not. He asked me if I had been scared and I replied that I hadn't. He told me that everything was O.K.; they were just the angels that the Lord has watching the church.

Bill Sproat

As the owner of the Pittman Trucking Lines, I sometimes have to fill in for a sick driver and deliver loads personally. This was the reason for my taking a particular load to Memphis. On my way back to Florida, the semi in which I was driving developed a major problem. I noticed in the rear-view mirror that the sides of the trailer had broken loose from the frame and were sagging over the wheels on the right side.

It was late Friday night and no mechanics were available, so I called my wife, Belinda, and asked her to pray for the trailer to hold. The trailer fell to half an inch above the tires. I knew it would be disastrous if it fell further, as all the tires would blow out and the trailer would come to an immediate halt.

In an effort to avoid a major accident and possibly kill someone, I exited the interstate highway and took back roads through Mississippi and Alabama, heading for Montgomery. The load I was carrying was dated, and I really needed to get to Florida on time.

I called Belinda again to tell her how I was doing and that I would call her again in the next town. She told me that she and her friend, Cindy Shaw, had been praying for angels to help stabilize the trailer.

About 11:30 I glanced in the mirror to see if it had dropped any further, and to my surprise saw a huge angel holding up the rear of the trailer. I blinked, because I had been up since very early the previous morning and was very tired, but when I looked again, he was still there! I said out loud, "If you'll hold it up till I get to Montgomery, I'll get some rest."

I stopped at a convenience store with a well-lit area beside it and asked the cashier, who was behind a cage, if I could park there for a couple of hours. She said it would be all right, if I felt safe. I was so tired that I forgot to call Belinda again. I thanked God for keeping me safe thus far and slept in peace for two hours.

When I woke up, I found myself completely surrounded by pimps, drunks, prostitutes, and drug dealers. I had stopped right where they met after the bars closed down.

I got out, got myself some coffee, climbed back in, and pulled out from the store at 4:00 A.M. When I arrived home at 8:30, I told Belinda I had seen an angel.

Belinda told me that after I called her the last time, Cindy had called back to tell her not to worry. She had seen a vision of an angel holding the trailer off the tires. She was going to tell me, but I had failed to call her back.

Ronnie Pittman

5

Divine Instruction

It was October of 1975. As we opened the door we noticed that the house was too quiet. As the late afternoon sunshine spilled into the living room, it broke into a patchwork pattern on the gold carpet. We had expected our teenage daughter, Beverly, to welcome us at the door, but all that greeted us was dead silence.

I went to her room, thinking she might be resting. Instead, there I was faced with one of those situations that always happen to other people. I saw the note telling me she had run away from home and beside it the tresses of her beautiful, long, brown hair.

Questions and thoughts began to swirl in my mind: Where is she? Who is she with? How long has she been gone? Is she safe? This can't be! There is so much evil in this world. God, please don't let harm come to her.

We cried and prayed as hours passed. Each time the phone rang we frantically answered, hoping to hear her voice. No one knew what we were experiencing, and as we received our regular calls, we tried to remain calm and nonchalant, hoping the conversation would end quickly so the line would be clear for her call. Night was fast coming. "Please God, let me hear from her before dark. Please!"

I love the LORD, because he hath heard my voice and my supplications. Because he hath inclined his ear unto me, therefore will I call upon him as long as I live (Psalm 116:1-2).

Finally, the call came. She had spent hours at a shopping mall in a beauty shop trying to repair the damage she had done when she cut her hair.

This was the beautiful little girl whom I gave to God as a baby and trained in the way she should go. I saw her baptized in Jesus' name at an early age and filled with the Holy Ghost. She never missed a church service, and she was involved in all the activities of the church. But when the cancer of worldliness began eating at her spirit, I was not even aware of it. Now, as I looked at her, glaring back at me was the spirit of rebellion! It was time to do battle with this ugly, strong-willed spirit.

For we wrestle not against flesh and blood, but against principalities, against powers, against the rulers of the darkness of this world, against spiritual wickedness in high places (Ephesians 6:12).

I prepared for battle. "Am I dressed properly?" I asked myself. I had truth, righteousness, the preparation of the gospel of peace, the helmet of salvation, and the sword of the Spirit. But something was missing: my shield of faith. Frantically I searched my heart for it, but I could not find it. I knew I had to have it to win this most important battle with Satan.

The next week was a busy one, because we were having a citywide crusade reaching for souls. Satan was there also, with his slurs and snares: "Reach a city? You can't even reach your own daughter!"

After much prayer and many tears, there seemed to be no change in Beverly's attitude. Each day she was more withdrawn and stronger willed. Rebellion had its ugly fingers clenched with a death grip.

As the first service of the crusade began on Wednesday night in the city auditorium, the crowds came, and we sang and worshiped and praised God. There she was: a girl who had once danced in the Spirit and worshiped God, but so different now. She stood with face drawn, arms folded, and mouth clenched in defiance.

As Thursday and Friday nights came, I thought, Surely it will happen tonight. God, save my girl. Don't let her be lost. I kept hoping for a change, but I still had not located my lost piece of armor—my shield of faith.

If it did not happen Wednesday, Thursday, or

Friday, then it had to be Saturday, because that was the last night of the crusade. The ex-hippies testifying in the services told everyone that the world had nothing to offer but loneliness, emptiness, and pain. Surely she would listen to them, because they had come out of a world that she was looking at with such longing. Saturday night came to a close, and much to my disappointment, my daughter seemingly had not been touched.

I went home bone-weary, tired, and disappointed. For weeks we had worked so hard sending out announcements, having special choir practices, and doing all the things it takes to produce a big crusade. I collapsed into bed about midnight. At 2:00 A.M., I was awakened by the presence of God and a still, small voice whispering in my ear. "If you will get up and go pray for Beverly, I will answer your prayer."

Tired and weary as I was, I somehow received strength to get up and walk to her room. As I walked into her room, I found it—my shield of faith. I hugged it tightly to my chest and walked over to her bed. Stretching my hand over her head, I said, "In Jesus' name, it is done!"

She did not awaken, but there arose such faith in my soul as I had never experienced before. A wheel of joy flipped over in my soul and replaced the heaviness. Peacefully, I went back to bed and slept soundly until morning.

As the first rays of sunlight filtered through the curtains, doubt and heaviness began to attack me, but I remembered the words of the Lord. "If you will get up and go pray for Beverly, I will answer your prayer." Faith took over once again. With renewed confidence I said aloud, "I rebuke you, Satan, in Jesus' name. God has given me this day, and you will not take it from me!"

There was a song in my heart as I prepared for Sunday school. Faith was in action. As far as I was concerned, it had already happened. Satan had lost the battle and was on the run. The shield of faith gave me power to quench all the fiery darts of the wicked one, and it will do the same for anyone.

When I saw Beverly that morning, there seemed to be no change at all in her appearance. The rebellion seemed to be making a final stab, fighting back like a wounded animal. But that did not bother me, because in my heart all I could sing was, "It is finished, the battle is over. It is finished; there will be no more war. It is finished, the end of the conflict. It is finished, and Jesus is Lord!"

As church progressed that Sunday morning, my joy was more than I could contain. God's Spirit came over me, and I danced before the Lord with all my might. It was my victory march!

Had Beverly changed? No, not to those who only looked on the surface and saw her sullen, defiant personage. But I saw her through the eyes of faith as a radiant, submissive child of God.

Sunday afternoon passed by, and in prayer I said, "Lord, I don't care how You do it, but I make this one request. Let Beverly surrender of her own free will." I did not want anyone to beg her to go to the altar, but I wanted her to go at her own initiative.

I thanked God for a church that stood behind us during this time, praying, reaching, helping, encouraging us, and sharing our pain. And it also shared our victory as Beverly totally surrendered her life to God. The girl God gave back to us that night was much more full of the Spirit than she had ever been. Now she was changed completely, an example of God's miracle-working power. On the following Wednesday night as the altar service was given for those who had a need, Beverly was in the line. When D. L. Welch, her grandfather, prayed, victory came completely.

Certainly, rebellion attacked again but never completely possessed. When she fought battles in the future, Beverly was never too proud to reach for help, asking for prayer.

Years later I took great pride as a mother when I watched her walk down the altar to become Mrs. Curtis Parker. It was a beautiful wedding with white lace, candles, songs, and promises. I watched their car drive off into their happy-ever-after life, not knowing that only three months later, tragedy would make its mark on their lives.

It was on Thanksgiving Day during an early-morning hunting trip. A gun accidentally discharged, and Curtis was shot in the leg below the knee. When I should have been strong and encouraging her, it was Beverly who had the faith, the song in her heart, and the trust as she would daily say, "Mother, everything is going to be all right." The smile on her face gave me courage to make it. Two weeks later, after much mental anguish, the leg was amputated.

When my children returned to church a month later, they were called on to address the congregation. I shall never forget the praise she offered: "I thank God for trusting me through this trial."

Shirley Welch

Note: Shirley Welch is the founder of MAD (Mothers against the Devil) and the wife of Paul H. Welch, pastor of First Pentecostal Church, Pensacola, Florida.

Three times the Lord Jesus has spoken to me in an audible voice. Each time it has been something right out of the Bible that I was in need of.

The first time was after I had received the scriptural revelation of Jesus Christ and the plan of salvation and had promised Brother Welch that I would be over the next Sunday to be baptized in Jesus' name. Up till this time my family and I had been Baptists, but recently I had received the Holy Ghost, and the Spirit led me to an understanding of biblical truth.

That Sunday when I got home from work the kids ran out to meet me, saying, "Mother is not going to that church." I tried not to let my concern show, but the devil was telling me all the time that I would be attending one church and my family would be attending another. As I was getting ready and telling the Lord how bad the situation was, He said, "John, you have to love Me more than your family!"

I had recently read words like this in the Bible. I thanked the Lord for His words of encouragement and got baptized in Jesus' name. A few weeks later my wife and all my children were baptized and filled with the Holy Ghost.

The second time God spoke to me was after I had received the revelation of scriptural truth and was born again. I felt that most people would want to know what the Lord had shown me, especially those in other churches who had been misinformed. After witnessing for a few months and not having won anyone to the Lord, I became discouraged and told the Lord that no one wanted His truth.

The Lord spoke to me, "Keep sowing the seed, and someday it will fall on good ground!" I knew that the parable of the sower spoke about some seed falling on good ground. These words blessed me, and I kept sowing the Word of God. In a matter of a few months, seven souls that I had witnessed to entered the church family. Since that time, I have never been discouraged about witnessing for the Lord. Jesus knows who is the good ground, but we do not. If we sow the Word of God continually, we shall also reap.

The third time God spoke to me was during the inauguration of Richard Nixon, who had with him a well-known evangelist. The news commentators told what great friends they were and had many good things to say about the evangelist. I thought, Why don't they recognize great men like Brother Welch and others who know and tell the truth? The Lord spoke to me, "Woe unto you, when all men shall speak well of you!"

This statement sounded familiar, so I got out my Bible and started looking for it in the Scriptures. In Luke 6:26 Jesus said: "Woe unto you, when all men shall speak well of you! for so did their fathers to the false prophets."

The Lord has an answer for every question and problem that we might have, if only we will believe and ask him.

John E. Jackson

When my brother, Barry, and I were little, we stayed a lot with my great-grandmother. She took us to Sunday school and always tried to teach us what was right.

One night after we had all gone to bed, I was still awake and looked up to see a dark, glowing creature standing in the doorway. I knew that he was a demon. I was so terrified as he walked over to me that I could not even scream or speak! The creature put his hand over my mouth, and I couldn't breathe. I was suffocating.

Even though I could not speak, I prayed in my mind, "In Jesus' name, go away!" He took his hand away and moved across the little room to where my brother was sleeping.

I managed to get up and run to my great-grand-mother. Trembling in terror, I told her what had happened. She jumped out of bed, rebuking the demon in the name of Jesus and praying for my brother. I don't know if she could see the demon, but I still could. When Granny prayed, the creature ran by us and fled down the hall out of the house.

Although I am married and have two children of my own, I still recall that night and the power in a Christian grandmother's prayer for her little ones.

Ouida Smith

One Sunday after church, my husband, my three-year-old son, and I went with friends to Captain D's restaurant. The place was absolutely full and very noisy with dishes clanging and orders being shouted.

My son, Jason, told everyone at the table about the fish he caught when he and his dad went fishing the day before. When he held out his little hands to show the size of the fish, a lady at the next table interrupted.

Holding her hands out much bigger she asked, "Don't you mean this big?"

He quickly responded, "No ma'am! I go to Sunday school, and I don't lie. I can sing 'Jesus Loves Me,' too. Want to hear me?"

Politely the lady said yes, and Jason began to sing softly. The noise in the restaurant abruptly stopped as he sang. There were no dishes rattling, nobody talking, not even any noise coming from the kitchen. It was as if he was using a microphone, even though his voice was gentle and soft. Such an awesome presence of the Holy Spirit was in the room that after he had finished singing, one lady asked, "Did you feel that?"

I can't give you the name of the person or the problem, but I am convinced that someone in the room needed to hear that Jesus loved him or her. God used the tenderness of a little child to minister to someone who possibly would not have been receptive if hearing the message from an adult.

Belinda Pittman

6

Warning

In August 1993 my daughter, Whitney, and I went shopping at a local department store. We were purchasing a gift for my dearest friend and former classmate, Martha.

Since Martha and I have birthdays one week apart, it has remained our tradition through our twenty-five-plus years of friendship to celebrate with a special lunch and gift exchange. This was the day for that luncheon.

When Whitney and I finished our shopping, we returned to the car to stuff the gift bag and sign the card. As I dutifully wrote my best wishes for a happy birthday, I heard an audible voice say, "Lock the doors." The voice carried such authority that I reacted without hesitation, pressing the electric lock to secure the doors.

As I pressed the lock, I turned just in time to see a tall, thin, blond man poised to open the passenger door where my child sat. Apparently hearing the click of the lock, he withdrew his hand, hesitated a moment, and then put his hand out again as if to try the handle.

It took me several seconds to comprehend that this man was actually trying to get into my car, but it didn't take me any longer than that to call upon the name of Jesus.

The man immediately stepped back, leaning against the truck next to us. He stood there for four or five seconds, flipped a cigarette ash, and then walked around to a car several spaces down. Leaning against the car, he crossed his arms and gave me a long, hideous stare.

I know not what this man's intentions were. While I felt a chill at the incident, I also felt an overwhelming security that God loved me so much to warn me at precisely the right moment.

What a testimony this incident is to my child! I could tell her day after day of God's promise to protect us, but now that she has experienced that protection, she will never have a doubt that His promise is true.

I heard a warning from God another time also. We had sold our home and were looking to purchase one much nearer to church because we spend so much of our time there. The gentleman who had bought our home was a physician coming from across the country, and he needed to take occupancy within a week.

It was quite a task trying to get so many things

packed and moved out in such a short period of time, especially when we had no place lined up to move to temporarily. My parents were spending most of their time at their condominium on the Gulf of Mexico and graciously offered to let us move into their house in town. Not wanting to make a hasty decision about purchasing a new home, we accepted their offer.

One night during our stay, I was awakened by someone calling my name. I thought it was my husband, but realizing that he was still asleep, I decided that I must have been dreaming.

Turning to adjust my pillow, I again heard the voice behind me say, "Becky, get up and go out!" I was startled but not frightened at all. Not sure what the warning meant, I hesitated for a moment.

The third time the voice was not so gentle. "Becky, get up and go out now. The smoke alarms are not working. Do not ignore this, or you will die!" I wasted no time leaving the bed!

I ran into the hall checking every room upstairs, but neither seeing nor smelling any signs of fire, I quickly dashed downstairs. Still, I could find nothing out of the ordinary. Praying for direction, I turned to see a tiny glow from the power light on the dishwasher.

Flipping on the kitchen light, I found the dishwasher stuck on the dry cycle. The entire unit was extremely hot. No doubt, had I not been warned, it would shortly have been in flames.

By the way, I did check the smoke alarms, and none of them worked!

One Sunday evening Charlie had to be at church for musicians practice an hour earlier than I needed to be there for choir practice. On the way there, his truck overheated. Stopping to put water in the radiator, he tried unsuccessfully to get the cap off. The cap had a double click on it before it would open. Knowing he had already passed the first click, he felt impressed to move to the side to get a better grip.

When he reached the second click, the cap, under pressure, flew off. It shot about fifteen feet, followed by a surge of steam. Without question, had he remained in the front, he would have been severely burned or injured from the force of the cap blowing off.

Sometimes warnings come in the form of subtle thoughts, sometimes in more notable ways. However they come, it is to our benefit to be sensitive to the Spirit and the voice of God.

Becky McQuaig

And thine ears shall hear a word behind thee, saying, This is the way, walk ye in it, when ye turn to the right hand, and when ye turn to the left (Isaiah 30:21).

The beloved of the LORD shall dwell in safety by him; and the LORD shall cover him all the day long, and he shall dwell between his shoulders (Deuteronomy 33:12).

Because thou hast made the LORD, which is my refuge, even the most High, thy habitation; there shall no evil befall thee, neither shall any plague come nigh thy dwelling (Psalm 91:9-10).

But whoso hearkeneth unto me shall dwell safely, and shall be quiet from fear of evil (Proverbs 1:33).

By faith Noah, being warned of God of things not seen as yet, moved with fear, prepared an ark to the saving of his house (Hebrews 11:7).

This book records only a few of the miraculous workings of the Lord among His people. It is, of necessity, an abridged account. Though it omits much detail, I trust and hope that the magnitude of the Lord's intervention will be evident.

In my early days as a Christian, it was my great good fortune to be chauffeur and traveling companion for some three years to D. L. Welch. On one occasion, my wife and I drove Brother Welch to Orange, Texas, where we left him to visit his friend, Brother Gamblin, and we proceeded on to Houston. There, we looked up estranged friends whom my wife had known since childhood. Our hope was to share with them the great transformation that God had worked in our lives in delivering us from the drug scene of the sixties and early seventies. We had no idea what we were walking into.

Our friends, Dale and Diane, had two small children under five years old, both of whom were Diane's from a previous marriage. The father, who had given up all rights to the children, had been persuaded by his current girlfriend to kidnap the children.

We arrived at their apartment late at night and were informed of the situation. The very next morning three large, belligerent men (including the ex-husband) and a woman (the instigator of the whole conspiracy and at least as belligerent as the men) kicked in the front door of the apartment, presumably to take the children.

I was upstairs with the children, including my own little girl, who was five years old. I had seen from an upstairs window the intruders running toward the front door and knew what was happening. My thoughts were: (1) My daughter is up here with these children and is apt to be taken or harmed. (2) Dale, who is downstairs with his wife, and Fran (my wife) are smaller in stature than I, who am hard pressed to cast a noticeable shadow. Therefore, the intruders will make short work of them and come quickly up the stairs to take the kids. (3) The stairway is very narrow and will only allow one person at a time to ascend. (4) I need a large stick with which to welcome them at the top of the stairs.

I came up with plan A: I pulled a leg off a portable crib and had a nice, three-foot piece of oak with which to crack skulls. I waited at the top of the stairs but no one came. I learned later that Dale had taken a few karate lessons and was able to put up a good fight, so the intruders had a bit of trouble with him. I decided to move to plan B: go down and help Dale. Club in hand, I started down the stairway.

The Holy Ghost came upon me. My arms went limp, so that I could not lift them, and the Lord spoke to me, "There is no way that I would do in this circumstance what you are intent on doing." With this statement came a flood of understanding of what He was saying to me.

First, since I am a Christian, Jesus is my example, so I am to strive to do as He would in every situation. At the time, I had no clue as to what that might be, only that what I was doing was wrong.

Second, how would I tell Dale and Diane of the great and mighty God in whom I profess to believe so strongly and of His "very present help in trouble" (Psalm 46:1) if I opposed His Word with my actions, regardless of the circumstance? It was going to be difficult to find a translation of the Scriptures that included "cracking skulls" among the fruit of the Spirit.

Third, abandoning plan B seemed the prudent thing to do, since I could not lift the club.

The first thing I could think of was to call the police, but upon picking up the phone I found that my wife was on an extension doing that very thing. Then, I decided to express my concerns to the Lord. I told the Lord that I could understand His expecting *me* to take a beating, but these guys were not beating me, they were beating Dale. How could I expect Dale to believe that it was God's will for him to be beaten and that I could not help because I was a Christian? That would not be a very good advertisement for Christianity. I told the Lord that the situation was His, but whatever He was going to do, He had to do immediately, because Dale was being hurt. I leaned my stick against the wall and started back down the stairs.

As I descended the stairs I saw that the three men had finally managed to pin Dale's arms, and the largest of the three had his fist drawn back for what would be a devastating blow. Then, for no apparent reason, a look of sheer terror simultaneously came upon the faces of all three of the men. They released Dale and ran out the door, the woman following closely behind. In an instant the nightmare was over.

At this point I was wondering what I could say to Dale to explain why I hadn't immediately rushed down the stairs to help him. Should I say, "Well, Dale, I figured I'd let you surround 'em while God and I were upstairs discussing proper etiquette for the situation"? It didn't sound like something he would understand.

But the Lord took care of every part of the circumstance. Not only had He protected our witness by handling the intruders and keeping me from doing the wrong thing, but He had protected Dale, who was not hurt in the fight and only suffered broken eyeglasses. He had protected Dale's wife and my wife and all our children. And He had protected me, who might have had a three-foot oak stick shoved down my throat.

In addition, before I could begin to explain from my point of view what had happened, Dale immediately said he knew that "Big Daddy" (his term for God) had worked a miracle for him and his family because Fran and I were there. The Lord had already made it unnecessary for me to explain or defend what I did in obedience to Him.

The Lord Jesus was complete to the last detail in His handling of the situation. All I had to do was to make the decision not to do the wrong thing, which was all I knew to do, and believe and allow Him to work.

Someday in eternity, when I have a private audience with the Lord, I intend to ask Him just what those men saw that so completely terrified them. It must have been really something.

This situation was as intense and life threatening as I ever hope to encounter. During my twenty-two years of living for the Lord, He has shown Himself mighty in my behalf in countless miracles of every sort: healings, financial rescues and blessings, deliverance from impossible situations, and so on. I chose to share this experience because it is unique.

Newman Gersin

One night, I dreamed that a man and woman came to our front door. They were drunk and carried a gun, intending to harm us. Then I awoke to someone's banging on our front door. It was about 3:00 A.M.

My husband went to the door and was about to open it. I emphatically told him not to open the door, relating to him the dream I had just had.

The people outside were in a drunken rage and

thought that we were the people who had lived in the house before Jim and I had moved in. They were very determined to gain entrance into our home. After much talking, we convinced them to go away.

I am sure that God warned us not to open the door. Those people would have shot first and asked questions later. The Lord is still our protector!

Liza Kiesling

One night about 2:00 A.M., I was sitting all alone in the living room, unable to sleep. I had resigned my job the day before and was making plans to apply for another position.

As I sat quietly in my recliner, all at once a bright light shone in the living room. Something spoke to my mind, "Take your family and belongings and move away from this area. There is a hurricane coming soon that will damage most of this region."

The message was so intense and direct that I went into the back bedroom of my trailer and awakened my mother. I told her what had happened, and we sat up the rest of the early morning hours discussing the warning and planning our move.

Around 9:00 A.M. I called a moving company to set up a date to pack and move to Pensacola. I withdrew my savings from the bank, and my family and I went on to Pensacola to find a house to rent. We stayed a few days, found a nice place to live, and then returned to Louisiana, where a few days later the moving company came and moved us out.

Eleven days after we returned to Pensacola, Hurricane Camille struck Venice, Louisiana, the place we had moved from, and destroyed almost everything standing! When I returned to check on my home and trailer I was shocked to discover that they were both gone! The only thing left was one small bathroom sink, lying on the ground. It was the only remaining item on one and a half acres of land!

Our God is real! He warned us in time and saved our lives. My mother, who was not a Christian at that time, later gave her heart to the Lord. If she had died in Hurricane Camille she would have been lost spiritually.

Our Lord could see years beyond and allowed her this time to be saved. I praise His holy, wonderful name again, and thank Him for saving our lives.

Carolyn Smith

One night I had a very disturbing dream. I saw a young boy fall from a balcony and watched as he tumbled toward the pavement below. I knew when he hit that he would be crushed, but all I could do was watch. I didn't see him hit, but I did see some people pick up the limp body and carry it away.

Later, I again dreamed about the boy falling off the balcony, only this time I was very close to him. As he fell, he looked up and said to me, "I'm just a child!" I felt so helpless. I woke up and was so upset that I began to pray: "God, if there is a child in danger, please help him!" I prayed about the dream for some time and thought about it for days.

About a week later, there was a news report about a child in Destin. A day earlier, he had fallen from the balcony of a condominium where his family was staying. He had climbed up the rail and fallen eight stories to the asphalt below, sustaining only a scratch on his cheek.

His mother stated that an angel had caught him. Everyone, including the rescue personnel, confessed that it was a miracle.

Although the child in my dream was a little older, the balcony looked the same. God had spared this child! After I heard about this child, the burden of the dream left me.

Pam Vaughn

When we were living in Canberra, Australia, my husband, John, was a civil engineer and owned an earth-moving company. He was working about two miles from our house on a job, clearing a thousand acres of brush so a pine forest could be planted.

Because it was winter and very cold, I would take him a hot meal at lunch. One morning, John told me not to bother with lunch. Since his mother and elderly aunts were visiting at the time, he had decided to knock off work early and come home to have dinner with the family.

As the morning wore on, I had an uneasy feeling that I couldn't shake, so I loaded the kids, my mother-in-law, and John's aunts into the car and drove to the area being cleared. His family wanted to see it anyway, so I figured that was a good excuse to check on John.

I still had the uneasy feeling. When I reached the top of the hill, for some reason I turned the car around, facing toward the road back down.

As soon as I saw the bulldozer running but did not see John, I knew that there was a problem. Trying to remain calm, but fearing the worst, I left my three-year-old daughter, Kelly, with my mother-in-law and aunts and took my ten-year-old son, Danny, with me to look for my husband.

As we walked down the steep hill to the bulldozer, I became queasy and short of breath in anticipation of what we would find. My son climbed to the top of a large cluster of boulders and looked down the other side. He spotted his dad pinned beneath a huge tree that he had been cutting down with a chainsaw. When the tree fell, it bounced off a boulder and fell back into John's chest, knocking him down. The accident had happened about 9:00 A.M., and it was now noon.

Since he was working alone in this area and

remembered that he had told me not to come up, John viewed the situation as hopeless. We all burst into tears and then tried to figure out a way to get him out from under the tree.

I first shut the bulldozer off, giving John a welcome break from the noise. Before we arrived, he had somehow managed to start the chainsaw while on his back and to cut a big notch out of the tree that pinned his leg. To his dismay, however, the saw had run out of gas. I refilled the saw with gas, but each time I tried to cut, it jammed and died.

We sent Danny back up the hill to tell his grandmother where to find the other workers and to get Life Flight, because we were thirty miles from the nearest town.

I cleared the sawdust and debris from John's feet to better evaluate the situation and see how bad he was bleeding. Only then did I realize how blessed we were that he had run out of gas, preventing him from cutting further into the tree. His legs were so severely twisted that had he continued to cut, he would have amputated his own feet at the ankles.

John was quickly going into shock, and I was helpless. Finally, the helicopter along with other workers arrived at the scene. First, rescuers quickly cut large chunks out of the tree in an effort to get it off his chest so that he could breath easier. Then they freed his mangled legs.

He had a broken pelvis, a fractured femur, nerve damage in one leg, and multiple cuts. He spent seven weeks in the hospital and had two lengthy surgeries.

A week after he came home, I drove up to the accident site and retrieved a chunk of the tree for my garden. It was the end of the tree where he had carved, "I love you," when he thought he was going to die in his predicament.

It's amazing how precious things become when it seems that you are going to lose them. I thank God for giving me that uneasy feeling and for sparing the father of my children.

Jeanne Sweeney

In February 1985 I dreamed that an angel escorted me to a staircase and told me to sit there. A few moments later he showed me the top step, which was cracked. The step then opened up, and the angel told me to look through it. When I did, I saw only never-ending darkness. Then the step closed up, still leaving the visible crack.

Off in the distance I could hear people coming. Even though I could not see them, I knew that they were walking very carelessly, believing that the ground under them was secure. The angel told me that I had to stop them and warn them about the step. If I did not, they would step on it, fall through, and be lost forever.

To this my reply was, "How? Look at who these

people are, and I'm just a nobody. No one will listen to me!" I was then reminded about the step and their fate if I didn't tell them. As I stood there trying to figure out what to say to make them listen to me, I could hear them getting really close. I became very worried because my time was running out. Then the dream ended!

As I thought about the dream, I asked God what it all meant and who the people were. I did not receive an answer, so I just held the dream close to my heart and thought on it from time to time.

Later, while sitting in church and listening to the sermon, I felt the presence of the Lord. He said to me, "Your dream is not as you supposed it to be. These are *My* people. They are not walking in sincerity. They think they have it made, but they don't. These are the ones who have not completely given themselves to me! They still play with and entertain worldly desires. These are the ones who through battles have become weak and because of no intercessor have lost their battle and have given up. These are the backsliders. They are *My* people! They have been baptized in *My* name and have received *My* Spirit. They must be awakened! They must be brought back into the fold, for time is short. Pray for them, fast for them, intercede for them!"

After returning home from a recent ladies retreat I was unable to go to sleep that first night. Still pumped up and in total awe over what God had done for me, I stayed up to give Him praise. After a time of prayer, I went to bed and had another dream. This one was short but intense.

I was standing in a dark room, engaged in a very strong and severe spiritual battle and speaking in tongues as I had never done before. The battle was so great that it took every ounce of strength I had. Still I could not stop. As I awoke from the dream, my body was still trembling. While I lay there thinking about what had just happened, the Lord revealed to me what it was all about.

"This is the only way that the battles can be won. You must war fervently with all diligence. You must war like this: 'The effectual fervent prayer of a righteous man availeth much.' This is the only way to pull down the strongholds of Satan. Warfare is strong and powerful and entails every bit of you. Are you willing to submit? I have need of you!"

Sue Malkoch

7

Sustaining Grace

There comes a time in all of our lives when we face situations that we do not understand. It is a time when we must dig in our heels and endure.

Sometimes things don't make sense, at least not for the moment. We look at others' situations and say, "It won't happen to me," but it does. It may be the death of a child, a fire that destroys all our possessions, a disease that painfully eats away at a loved one, or our own affliction that makes living so difficult. It might be an accident that in a split second changes life forever, a financial devastation, or the birth of a child with a very special need.

In all these things God gives sustaining grace. As Christians, we have the assurance that God is in control of every situation we encounter and will sustain us through every trial.

The steps of a good man are ordered by the LORD: and he delighteth in his way. Though he fall, he shall not be utterly cast down: for the LORD upholdeth him with his hand (Psalm 37:23-24).

We may view these occurrences in our lives as tragedies, but we need to consider that our heavenly Father sees the whole picture. We are limited to the here and now, but He holds the future. What we may consider a personal tragedy may be a blessing in disguise. God knows what is best for us and what events are necessary to mold us and shape us into the kind of person He needs us to be in order to fulfill His perfect will. Another consideration is that our circumstance may often be for a witness or example to those around us. Whatever the reason for the situation, it is far better for us to trust God than to reason with our limited understanding.

Trust in the LORD with all thine heart; and lean not unto thine own understanding. In all thy ways acknowledge him, and He shall direct thy paths (Proverbs 3:5-6).

Charlie and I have two wonderful friends, Harry and Marie Bush. They have a son, Michael, who has Down's syndrome.

Michael requires constant supervision, has severe

health problems, and in general, takes up much of their time. He is the youngest of their children, the rest of whom are all married. Michael is eighteen. At a time when many of their friends enjoy having their children out of the nest, or at least old enough to care for themselves, Harry and Marie know they have one who will remain with them permanently.

Many would look on this situation as a problem, but those people don't know what a blessing and joy Michael is. This young man is a very special gift from God. He literally is the only person I know who has no hatred. He is very tenderhearted, polite, and kind. He's extremely patient, especially when he visits my home and has to endure my little girl's tea parties.

He loves and accepts people for what they are. He's not a friend because of what he gains from the friendship but rather because he wants to be. He hugs me and gives me a big smile every time I see him. We laugh together, we pray together, and we color together.

I'm glad that Michael is the way he is, because he shows me the innocence and purity of motive that God desires in all our lives. I've watched him many times during church services. He gives one hundred percent in worship and song. He welcomes and shakes hands with the visitors, and freely shares whatever he has with all the little children that flock around him.

One of the greatest lessons I've learned through Michael came during a Friday night youth service at our church. Michael played his harmonica and did a very good job; I saw a boy who used his one little talent to give God glory. I felt ashamed to think I have numerous resources at my disposal, yet I withhold.

I know it isn't easy raising a handicapped child, and at times Michael's parents wonder why God allowed this situation. But I also know they have put their trust in a loving God and are willing to accept whatever He has designed for their lives.

We all need to remember that when our lives look like a jigsaw puzzle and we have no clue where the pieces fit, God knows how it will look when completed.

It was lying on the table
in what seemed a thousand pieces.
I watched the little girl
as she tried to force the puzzle.
Never looking at the picture,
she cried in desperation.
Then I realized that she was I,
and her puzzle was my life.

Sometimes I hold a piece
and wonder where it goes.
Why can't I find a mountaintop,
the sunshine, or the rose?
But as the pieces come together,
I see with my own eyes,
If there were no shadows,
I would not see the light.

Jesus sees it all,
and He knows just where each little
       piece belongs.
Jesus sees it all,
and if I'll only let Him,
He will make my life a portrait
of His grace and of His mercy.
My Jesus sees it all.

by Becky McQuaig

There is a very special story that we have saved until last. It is authored by a man of distinction who has committed his entire life to the ministry of Jesus Christ—Nathaniel A. Urshan, general superintendent, United Pentecostal Church International. We would like to extend to Reverend Urshan a special thanks for his permission to use this story, and for his years of friendship to our family.

It was a shock when the doctors told us she would live just six months. When I walked in the room to give the family the prognosis, I looked Sharon in the eye and told her the doctors had given us heavy news.

She said, "I know that. I am hurting so bad. But you taught us right, Dad." I asked her what she meant. She said, "You taught us in all things to give thanks."

When I told her she had only been given three to six months she said, "I think I'll have more time." She lived sixteen months beyond that. She did, during that sixteen months, more than she did in all her other years.

She got to the point where she could hardly walk and was mostly in the bed. One day she said to her husband, "Please take me to the house of God. I want to hear the people worshiping God again."

Her husband told her she was too weak, so she asked him just to fix it where she could lie down when she got there. She wanted to be in church.

When she got there, she was so lifted by the worship that she danced and praised God all over the front of the sanctuary.

Then she went back to a man who had been kind enough to bring his wife to church for thirty years but had never made a move toward God. She took him by the hand and told him that if he would serve God she would gladly die. The man ran to the altar and repented, was then baptized in the name of Jesus, and came up out of the water speaking in tongues.

In Sharon's weakness there was born a strength. At our weakest point, we do some of the greatest things for God.

Finally the time came that we were called to her bedside to say good-bye. As she was passing away, her husband held her by the hand. Suddenly, he began hollering in tongues. People hearing him came running from all over to see what was happening.

After Sharon died, I said to him, "I have heard you speak with tongues before, Carl, but never hollering like that."

His reply was, "You haven't seen what I have seen!" He then told me he saw her going through the gates of eternity above which was written: "NO MORE PAIN, NO MORE SORROW, NO MORE TEARS. GOD HAS MADE ALL THINGS NEW."

We have a hope beyond this veil of tears. This life is not all we have. In II Corinthians the apostle Paul saw and heard things in the third heaven that he could not express with the human tongue. After having the experience, he proclaimed a different outlook on how life treated him when he said in II Corinthians 12:10: "Therefore I take pleasure in infirmities, in reproaches, in necessities, in persecutions, in distresses for Christ's sake: for when I am weak, then am I strong."

When we look at life in the comparison of what troubles we have here to what we stand to gain in the beauties of our eternal home, we can meet any existing position in life and win.

Nathaniel A. Urshan
(General Superintendent,
United Pentecostal Church International)

Eye hath not seen, nor ear heard, neither have entered into the heart of man, the things which God hath prepared for them that love him. But God hath revealed them unto us by his Spirit (I Corinthians 2:9-10).

There is a heaven, and there is a God who soon will be returning for His bride (the church).

No matter how dark the day, no matter what troubles or pain we must endure in this life, it is worth every sorrow we bear when we get a clear view of what is to come . . . to live forever and ever with our Lord and Savior Jesus Christ.

To Him alone be blessing and honor and glory and praises forever. AMEN.

Becky McQuaig

This is not the end.

Miracles are still taking place....

It Happens All the Time!

About the Authors

Charles and Becky McQuaig attend First Pentecostal Church, Pensacola, Florida, where Paul H. Welch is pastor and where they have been members all their lives. They are active in the Sunday school, music, choir, and drama departments. They have written two plays and a musical. Becky has authored several children's stories, and together they have written over thirty songs. They have been married twenty-five years and have a beautiful daughter, Whitney. Charles is a CAD draftsman and mechanical designer. Becky is a licensed surgical nurse.